Praise for Talent Magnetism

"*Talent Magnetism* is the missing book from most executive shelves. We have works on finance, marketing, operations, and research. But the engine that drives all of these areas needs talent for fuel, and Roberta Matuson can help you find and maximize the horsepower from that fuel. This book should be first before all others."

—Alan Weiss, PhD, Author of *Million Dollar C   'ting, The ⌐   oks.

"With her signature humor an   Roberta guides you through the   :e 'magnetic' to attract true super   know when to set them free. Th   ᵤᵤᵤ, but always informative and brutally honest, guide presents achievable steps to help even the most stodgy of institutions move and shake with today's talent pool. Because of her writing style it doesn't feel like you are reading a 'business guide book' and might even be something you choose to read twice just in case you missed something the first time through! If you find yourself in an organization where your employees act more like anchors than turbo charged engines driving your business towards success, start reading now!"

—Andrew Ashley, Vice President, Bank of America

"Roberta Matuson's insight has effectively provided us the blueprint for transforming our human capital from mediocre to magnetic, thereby attracting the *right* talent for our organization! *Talent Magnetism* is a must read for the CEO and HR professional that believes in the old 'business as usual' human capital strategy will sustain their organizational needs in today's talent scarcity."

—Joanne Berwald, Vice President of Corporate Human Resources, Mestek, Inc.

"Talent Magnetism is an exhilarating book. The workplace is ever-changing and Roberta continues to capture this in Talent Magnetism by sharing best practices and key recommendations to stay ahead of the game."

—Mary L. Froehlich, COO, Sydney Associates, Inc.

"Roberta Matuson does a masterful job of de-mystifying a critically important topic that eludes so many companies. This book is both a call to action and a prescription for success, complete with specific qualities that make companies talent magnets, and live examples of individuals and organizations that have successfully adopted those qualities. This is a 'must read' for anyone who is interested in creating an enterprise that consistently attracts and, more importantly, retains great people who will truly make a difference."

—Jerel Golub, President, CEO, Price Chopper Supermarkets

"The hiring pool is changing rapidly in the US and this is changing the DNA of our organizations. *Talent Magnetism* provides key principles on who to hire, motivate, retain and lead teams in this new world economy."

—Matthew Androski, Vice President GM America Sales at Mindjet

Talent Magnetism

How to Build a Workplace That
Attracts and *Keeps* the *Best*

ROBERTA CHINSKY MATUSON

NICHOLAS BREALEY
PUBLISHING

BOSTON • LONDON

First published in the United States of America and
Great Britain by Nicholas Brealey Publishing in 2013

20 Park Plaza, Suite 610	3-5 Spafield Street, Clerkenwell
Boston, MA 02116 USA	London, EC1R 4QB, UK
Tel: + 617-523-3801	Tel: +44-(0)-207-239-0360
Fax: + 617-523-3708	Fax: +44-(0)-207-239-0370

www.nicholasbrealey.com

Printed in the United States of America
18 17 16 15 14 13   1 2 3 4 5 6 7 8 9 10

ISBN: 978-1-85788-598-9

Library of Congress Cataloging-in-Publication Data

Matuson, Roberta Chinsky.
    Talent magnetism : how to build a workplace that attracts and
keeps the best / by Roberta Matuson.
        pages cm
    ISBN 978-1-85788-598-9 (pbk. : alk. paper) —
    ISBN 978-1-85788-932-1 (ebook)
    1. Employees—Recruiting.   2. Employment interviewing.
3. Employee selection.   4. Employee retention.   I. Title.
    HF5549.5.R44M383 2013
    658.3'1—dc23
                                                    2013018030

DEDICATION

This book is dedicated to my husband Ron, who has kept our lives going so that I could complete this book with time to spare, and to my children Zach and Alexis who are magnetic in every way.

ACKNOWLEDGEMENTS

I'd like to thank my agent, Linda Konner, for representing me and for her continued encouragement and support. I'd like to thank Nick Brealey for working directly with me to craft this book and for his priceless insight into an industry that at times feels like another universe to me. I'd also like to acknowledge my editor, Susannah Lear, and Nicholas Brealey's sales guru, Chuck Dresner, who somehow manages to keep his sense of humor through thick and thin. A big thank you also goes out to the entire Nicholas Brealey staff for their continued support.

My deepest gratitude goes to my mentor, Alan Weiss, who has always challenged me to think big and encouraged me to share my thought leadership with others.

I'd also like to thank all of the magnetic leaders who so willingly shared their stories. I hope they inspire you to be the type of leader that attracts and keeps the best!

CONTENTS

Talent Magnetism

This book is about attracting and retaining the best people—top talent—rather than pulling in the masses to fill open job requisitions. Why? Because you don't need a lot of people when you have a lot of talent.

So what is top talent? For the purposes of this book, I'm defining top talent as those people who are truly extraordinary, people who model behaviors you wish every employee would have. They're tops in their field (if not necessarily at the top of your organization), and they expect their employers will be at the top of their game as well. They are the ones who relentlessly drive the business forward.

You've certainly worked with some of these people throughout your career; if you are lucky, you have many of them in your organization right now. They are the people who take on the lion's share of the work without being asked, the ones who pick up the slack, and the ones who you can always count on when deadlines are tight. They are the people who are constantly looking for ways to improve their performance, while consistently achieving results. Often, they are the reason your company is still in business, in spite of tough economic conditions, and they are the reason you are prospering when others in your industry are barely making payroll.

But beware complacency. I've worked in a number of companies that mistakenly believed top talent would stick around if the firm made it seemingly impossible to leave. Stock options were given out freely, like candy dispensed on Halloween. That was all fine and good until the company earnings and the value of the stock tanked and the options were underwater.

Today's workers are wiser than they used to be. Some have experienced what it's like to be rightsized (the politically correct way of saying downsized) or have watched their parents and friends slide from the middle class into bankruptcy. What's more, a new generation of workers has come onboard, and these workers value personal time and the ability to make the world a better place as much as, if not more than, personal wealth and material possessions. Throwing more money at these people to get them in the door, along with the promise of a richer life if they stick it out, is no longer an effective recruitment or retention strategy. The workforce has changed, and so must you.

In my consulting practice, I've helped Fortune 500 companies across all industries, as well as small and medium-sized businesses, achieve dramatic growth and market leadership through talent magnetism. I've been fortunate to work with world-class companies, including Best Buy, Inc., New York Life, and New Balance, as well as many up-and-coming businesses. My most successful clients never simply say, "Our people are our most important asset." Instead, they demonstrate this principle every day with every decision they make.

Before you start worrying that you may not be up to this challenge, understand that many of my clients felt the same way until we began working together to create what I call a "magnetic workplace"—an environment where employees are passionate about their work and where customers love to do business. All that is required from you to begin is commitment and the desire to succeed.

Throughout this book I will guide you through the process that I've undertaken with many of my clients, large and small. I will share best practices from my clients and executives with the hope that you will incorporate many of these ideas into your business so you can achieve similar results. I'll provide case studies and tools you can use to create the stickiness that will keep your people connected to your organization. In addition, I'll end each chapter with a key recommendation for you to consider, which I'm calling the "rule of attraction." This is my "if you only do one thing" recommendation to help propel you forward at warp speed.

As we begin this journey together, keep in mind that as business conditions continue to pick up in many sectors, attracting and retaining top talent will become more challenging, especially if you choose not to take immediate action. With economic improvement comes an increase in hiring, which means workers will have more choices when deciding where to work. At the same time, an aging workforce means that many people will be changing gears and choosing to slow down or retire. Those of you who take action today and make acquiring and retaining top talent a priority will have the clear advantage, as you will have established yourself as the type of employer that others would be lucky to work for. Your magnetic pull will become the envy of those who missed the boat completely and those who were still operating under the belief that stock options could buy loyalty.

It's up to you as business owner, CEO, or senior executive to create the type of workplace that attracts, recruits, and retains top talent and repels mediocrity; it's up to you to create a corporate culture that values excellence.

Some of you may have inherited a culture that worked well in the 1980s but no longer works today. That's okay.

We'll discuss what's required in order to transform the culture, and I'll provide guidance along the way. Others of you are in the process of building your organizations and are sitting back as the culture begins to take shape. We'll discuss what you need to do to take control of this situation so that you are able to build a workplace that makes you and everyone else excited about coming to work every day.

We'll discuss company image and explore what you can do to attract top talent and customers to you—as well as how you can build a force field around your organization to prevent others from pulling talent away from you.

There will also be considerable discussion of employee retention, as too many employers mistakenly believe that pulling people into the organization and getting them to stick around require the same actions. If that were the case, employee turnover in most organizations would be dramatically lower than it is today.

As the business owner, CEO, or other senior executive, you are responsible to ensure that your management team knows that, when it comes to hiring, nothing but the best will do for your organization. You must hold this team accountable for recognizing and rewarding exceptional employees and for developing top talent, and you must make it part of their charge. You must also bring Human Resources into the fold so they work closely with you to enable talent magnetism.

The sooner you begin, the sooner you'll be able to reap the rewards of talent magnetism. Let's get started.

Workplace Magnetism

I remember the exact moment I met my dream employer. It was a springlike day in an otherwise dark time in my life. I was coming out of an abusive working relationship that I thought I would never recover from. But I knew that I had no choice but to persevere, as I only had myself to rely upon. I put on my happy interview face, pumped myself up, and prepared myself for what was to be the interview of a lifetime.

The moment I walked in the room, I knew we were destined for one another. The French call it *je ne sais quoi*, defined by Merriam-Webster Dictionary as "something that cannot be adequately described or expressed." I call it magnetism—that moment of irresistible attraction.

Our conversation (notice that I didn't say interview) reminded me of a waltz, where every move was in sync. An offer was made and I accepted it gladly. My boss later confided in me that the hiring committee had invited the other finalist in for one more interview, as they could no longer remember her after meeting me.

This is the power of magnetism—the pull that occurs when two entities are attracted to each other. It's interesting to note that I took this job even though the compensation being offered was significantly below market. That didn't matter to me. What did matter was the passion and enthusiasm of every person I met while interviewing. The commitment to being the best in the industry was evident throughout the organization.

Can you attract top talent without magnetism? Sure. But at what cost, and will these people stick around?

The feeling I described when I first walked through my future employer's door is exactly the feeling that your candidates will have if you are purposeful in the way you create your corporate culture. As you read through this book, keep in mind that every organization has the ability to create an environment where employees are happy and customers love to do business.

The Power of Workplace Magnetism

Being known as a talent magnet has a number of advantages. The first is that you will have your pick when it comes to employees. This is particularly important in tight employment markets, such as IT.

Think about companies like Google and Apple. Do you think they have a hard time getting the talent they need to fuel their growth? Are they out there begging their friends and family members for the names of people who know C++ or Java? Probably not.

Search online and you'll find dozens of articles about how to land a job at Google or Apple. That's because there are tons of applicants interested in working for companies with brands like theirs. It can be a hard pill to swallow, knowing that some companies have absolutely no problem finding candidates for jobs that are considered hard to fill, while others go hungry.

Magnetic Leader Raymond Pawlicki

G reat employees know other outstanding employees, and they aren't afraid to refer them to the companies they work for. No one knows this better than Raymond Pawlicki, senior VP and chief information officer (CIO) of Cambridge, Massachusetts–based Biogen Idec. Everyone knows that finding good information technology employees is as rare as finding snow in Florida. But not for Pawlicki. He's earned a reputation both inside and outside Biogen Idec for being the type of magnetic leader that others aspire to work for.

This kind of success didn't happen overnight. Pawlicki is extremely visible in both the information technology (IT) community and around town. "I speak at conferences as well as roundtables and talk about what it's like to work at Biogen," says Pawlicki. "It takes work. You have to be out there. You have to be willing to put at least 15 to 20 percent of your time into creating, understanding, and nurturing the culture and getting the word out there."

Pawlicki goes on to explain that doing so can be a real competitive advantage, especially when trying to fill positions in finance, research, and engineering, areas where good people are difficult to find. He notes that this commitment is not done often, nor is it done well. His reputation as a guy who really cares about his people makes it much easier to compete and win talent, especially when he's up against CIOs who either have poor reputations or no reputations at all. People don't hesitate to refer candidates to Pawlicki, which helps him avoid paying the hefty recruitment fees that others are forced to pay when hiring IT staff.

Likewise, mediocre employees know other mediocre employees and aren't afraid to bring them into the fold. This happens particularly in organizations where employees feel threatened. They know that if they bring in people who are better than they are, they may be asked to leave. So they do their best to make sure the status quo is maintained. Which group of employees would your rather have referring people to you?

Magnetic companies attract clients and customers to their brand with considerably less effort than nonmagnetic companies. People want to do business with magnetic organizations because of their stellar reputation, which is usually related to their employees. Examples of this can be found with brands like the Ritz-Carlton Hotel Company, which is known throughout the world for its gold standard of customer service. Many organizations try to emulate this company, which has allowed Ritz-Carlton to enter an entirely new line of business—advisory services and courses offered at The Ritz Carlton Leadership Center.

There are many more ways that magnetism impacts top-line growth, bottom-line profitability, and the overall health of an organization. I'll discuss this in more detail throughout this book.

Can Magnetism Be Bought?

Many people ask me if magnetism is something that can be bought. I don't believe it can be, though companies spend millions of dollars on PR firms every year trying to achieve this. Some companies falsely believe that receiving an award from the local chamber of commerce or being named among the "Best Companies to Work For" will magically cover blemishes that others know exist. The truth eventually breaks through.

Magnetism comes from within, and, thanks to the increased transparency afforded by the Internet, prospective candidates know when your company is trying to sell them a bill of goods. Today's jobs seekers are connected in ways that we could never have imagined. It takes about two seconds to see if you have a LinkedIn connection at a company you are considering. A simple Google search can reveal what really goes on in the bowels of the organization, as many people don't think twice about going public with their opinions. That can be a good thing if you have a workplace where people are fairly happy, but it can be a nightmare if you don't.

Roy Ng, senior vice president and head of business operations for the Cloud Business Unit at SAP, headquartered in Walldorf, Germany, believes that benefits, pay, and titles are still important to people. Ng reminds us of the importance of paying attention to all parts of employee packages, not just one factor. He says, "You can't simply do one well and be a great employer." He also notes that buying talent won't necessarily ensure that you'll be able to keep people. "If you can get to the heart of the person, you can pick up talent that you never thought you could." You must continuously work on strengthening your connections in order to keep these people. We'll go into more detail on how to do this in Chapter 13.

Where to Get Some Magnetism

Most companies have magnetism inside their organizations waiting to be released. Sometimes you have to dig down a few layers to find it, and other times it's on the surface for all to see. Of course, there are those situations where companies are unwittingly blocking the very candidates they are trying to pull in.

In those companies where recruiting top talent is a delegated "task," we often find a wall that prevents good people from penetrating the organization. Talent may be attracted, but at the same time they are unable to get past the wall put up by recruitment and hiring processes that no longer make sense or by managers who don't make the hiring process a priority. That's why it's so critical that, wherever possible, CEOs and other senior executives drive the recruitment process and check often to ensure any blockage is removed quickly.

Forward-thinking CEOs shop their businesses to make sure they know exactly what their customers are experiencing. I suggest you do the same when it comes to the experience of the job seeker. Begin by trying to apply for work in your own company. Are you tempted to give up along the way? If so, you most likely aren't alone. This is exactly what happens when highly sought-after candidates or passive candidates tire of the shenanigans that some employers put candidates through before they've had a chance to set foot in the door.

Being aware of the frustrations lurking in your application process will give you the opportunity to make necessary changes before you lose great candidates to the competition.

Finding Your Inner Magnetism

If you are having a difficult time determining what really attracts people to your organization, simply ask those who have recently joined your firm what initially drew them to your business. Then ask employees who've been with you a while why they choose to stay.

Sometimes people are more comfortable, and therefore more honest, when speaking to a third party about matters related to retention. That's where outside consultants can be beneficial. A good consultant knows when she is being given a stock answer and can probe further to get at the heart of the matter. She can also alert you to any patterns of unhappiness she may find along the way, which will give you the opportunity to rectify the situation before it's too late.

You may already know where your magnetism resides. I'm betting it's with some key leaders in your organization who closely resemble Pawlicki and Ng. Pay close attention to what they are purposely doing, and you may indeed be able to replicate that type of passion throughout your own organization.

What Good Is Attraction If You Can't Get Talent to Stick Around?

I've worked in organizations where we had no problems bringing good people in. That's because we had so much practice. We were running in place to replenish all the great people who kept leaving. Exhausting? Yes. Effective? No.

I see companies making significant investments in their recruitment programs yet doing little in the way of measuring employee happiness. What's the point of bringing in all these great people if you can't keep them? And what's the point of measuring employee happiness if you are not going to do anything with the data you've collected?

In the following chapter, we'll discuss how the workplace has changed over the past several years and what you can expect things to look like in the not-so-distant future. One thing we do know for sure, it's going to get a lot harder to keep the talent you have.

Rule of Attraction

Put yourself in the candidate's shoes and apply for a job with your company. How would you describe the experience? Was it simple and pleasant, or did you walk away frustrated? Take note of what worked and what didn't, and take action immediately to create an experience that is reflective of a world-class organization like yours.

CHAPTER

The Talent Pool Is Changing—Are You?

I keep hearing from CEOs and other senior executives how difficult it is to find good talent these days. I believe this is true. And you know what? This problem isn't going away anytime soon. In spite of the high unemployment numbers in some parts of the world, many positions are still going unfilled. In some cases, there appears to be a huge mismatch between the skills that people have and the skills that employers need.

In certain fields, this comes as no surprise. Take the tech industry as an example. It's estimated that by 2018 there will be some 1.4 million tech-related job openings in the United States, but the country will have only about 400,000 college grads to fill them. Technology is changing so rapidly that workers can't keep up. They may master one platform while in school only to find that companies require skills in a language that didn't exist when they began their training.

Even firms that aren't designing the next tablet are struggling. In a recently released study by recruiting firm ManpowerGroup, nearly half of U.S. employers surveyed said they're having trouble filling key jobs despite continued high unemployment. In Japan, 81 percent of respondents indicated that this is an issue. Notable shortages are also reported in other Asia Pacific markets, including Australia (50%), India (48%), and New Zealand (48%). In the Americas, the most urgent talent shortage is reported in Brazil, where 71 percent of employers identify difficulty sourcing employees with the relevant profile. The worldwide figure is 34 percent.

We've been hearing about the difficulty of filling positions in health care and engineering for a long time now. But many people would be surprised to find that organizations are coming up short when looking to hire sales reps, accounting and finance staff, drivers, and teachers. You may as well hang up your tools if you are looking to hire skilled workers like plumbers and electricians. The trades are losing their attraction among high school students, who are choosing careers that will allow them to stay in bed past 4:00 A.M. This is a huge problem for employers in need, as these jobs cannot simply be outsourced to workers in other countries.

This situation will only intensify as the economy improves and workers have more choices. At the same time, the baby boomers are finally retiring or moving into less demanding second careers. Now is the time to take action, and that's exactly what Lisa Hook, CEO of Neustar—a trusted provider of real-time information and analysis to the Internet, telecommunications, entertainment, advertising, and marketing industries throughout the world—is doing. Her company is planning for the future, to ensure there is a twenty-first-century workforce that is adequately trained.

In a recent *U.S. News Weekly* article, Hook wrote about how her company is investing in tomorrow's talent. She cites Neustar's heavy involvement in My Digital Life, a digital literacy program that teaches kids about technology and how to use it responsibly, which operates in both Virginia and Kentucky (the two states Neustar calls home). The company also participates in Year Up!, a one-year, intensive training program that provides low-income young adults with a combination of hands-on skill development, college credits, and corporate internships. Neustar also participates in the Anita Borg Institute's annual Grace Hopper Celebration event, which supports and promotes the advancement of women in technology.

Connecting with Tomorrow's Workers Today

Aquent is a leading global provider of specialized temporary staffing for high-end creatives and web experts. To keep up with the demand for talent with specific skills, the company is using the MOOC (Massive Open Online Course) model and applying this to the workplace.

Last summer, Aquent hosted its first-ever MOOC offering, Summer of Learning, a free, month-long HTML5 training course for marketing professionals. The course was created to address a documented skills gap among marketing professionals and to help the staffing firm place participants in hard-to-fill positions— like front-end developer and designer—that require HTML5 skills. More than 10,000 students took part in the course, and 150 of them were placed in positions with Aquent's client base immediately afterward.

"We understand the needs of building relationships today. The students today will be the managers hiring us ten years from now. We see this as part of our business lifecycle," states Alison Farmer, VP of learning and development at Aquent.

Think about what you can offer today to attract the workers you'll need to sustain and grow your business for years to come.

Neustar is continuing to build its pipeline. The company recently partnered with the University of Illinois at Urbana-Champaign to open the Neustar Labs Innovation Center, which enables university students to work with Neustar to develop commercial solutions to some of the most challenging problems customers face. The focus of the facility is on technology, information, and digital media. Working closely with Neustar Lab employees, students drive projects focused on open innovation while developing professional skills that cannot be taught in the classroom.

You can bet Neustar will have its eyes on rising talent and that participants will feel a connection to the organization that has provided them with the knowledge and experience that will significantly impact their lives for years to come.

Granted, not every company has the budget to sponsor an innovation center. That doesn't mean you can't be working today to attract tomorrow's talent. Consider introducing a program that encourages your employees to mentor those who show potential in areas where you know there will be a shortage of talent. Sponsor a club at your local university and become actively involved. This will provide you with a unique opportunity to nurture talent while making personal connections.

Talent Is Overrated—Or Is It?

The people who say talent is overrated are often the ones who have a tough time finding and keeping it. Or they've only experienced mediocrity, so they have no idea how different their organizations would be if they hired top talent. I can certainly understand this, as I used to believe that all tomatoes tasted the same. That was until I tried a tomato that came straight from the farm. If you believe talent is overrated, I suggest you be more selective the next time you have a bunch of candidates to choose from. I have a feeling you will become a convert, like me, to the difference that top quality can make.

Remember, I'm defining top talent as those people who are truly extraordinary. They model the behaviors you wish every employee would have. They can do the work of at least two people and they have no problem taking on vital projects without being asked. They are constantly striving for ways to better themselves while consistently achieving results and moving the company forward. In a nutshell, they "wow" your customers and clients as well as their coworkers. Do you still believe talent is overrated?

For a moment, imagine a workplace that has an abundance of talent on staff. Think about the possibilities! These high-achieving people can have an enormous impact on business results. Take, for example, a company like Disney. This conglomerate is known throughout the world for more than just animation. Everything it touches seems to turn to gold. The company's acquisitions, which include Pixar and Marvel, have added to its ranks of talented artists, engineers, and business innovators.

Compare Disney's successes with the trajectory of electronics retailer Circuit City, which made a conscious effort to disengage its top talent. The company did so by significantly reducing the pay of its top salespeople. Many defected and took jobs with competitors. Months later, Circuit City declared bankruptcy.

Why You May Lose Your Balance in the Coming Demographic Quake

Any conversation about the changing talent pool wouldn't be complete without a discussion on the graying of today's workforce. The pool of baby boomers in the workplace is shrinking, as many move into retirement or second careers. About 76 million people were born in the United States between

1946 and 1964. But only 46 million more are coming along in generation X, which follows the boomers. That gap is one of the things workforce planners worry about. Throughout 2009, Deloitte and Forbes Insights conducted Managing Talent in a Turbulent Economy, a five-part longitudinal survey of high-ranking executives worldwide. The report revealed that over the last decade, companies facing a skills shortage have been able to tap into the vast global talent markets such as China and India. But as Baby Boomers retire and skills grow scarce, there will be no additional Chinas or Indias coming online. A problem faced by many nations.

More than 10,000 baby boomers a day turn sixty-five, a pattern that will continue for the next nineteen years, according to the Pew Research Center. Traditionally, people retire in their early to mid-sixties. If that holds true, between 2013 and 2020, tens of millions of people will leave the workforce. Much has been written lately about people deferring retirement, often out of necessity (poor economy, shrinking retirement benefits, decimation of savings and retirement accounts, etc.) and working much later than their early to mid-sixties. What is not written about is the number of people who are forced to leave their jobs due to declining health, the need to care for an ailing partner, or relocations due to a spouse's retirement. Life-changing events are having an impact on both individuals as well as firms who employ them. A tremendous amount of knowledge will be walking out the door in a relatively short period of time. Will adequate replacements come along to pick up the slack?

I don't see how, unless someone figures out a way to birth or clone more gen Xers. We'll have to rely on technology to help us do more with fewer people. Companies will have to invest heavily in the development of their millennials (those born between 1982 and 2000) to ensure they have the bench strength to handle the additional responsibilities that will be thrust upon them. It's a good idea to plan now, so you'll be ready for the repercussions of the inevitable demographic shift.

Can you see why holding onto the talent you have is so critical?

Which End of the Pool Are You Standing In?

Some of you may be thinking that you'll be fine. Your employees are always telling you how much they love coming to work, or at least that's what you think they are saying. I recall a conversation I had with a CEO who had just received the results of a company-wide employee climate survey. He was absolutely dumbfounded by the findings. You see, weeks before receiving the report, he had paid a visit to each location and met individually with many of the employees. He told me they expressed gratitude for being employed by the company. He left his meetings feeling that his people were content. Clearly this wasn't the case, based on the consistently negative feedback he was holding in his hand. I told him not to confuse people telling you they are happy to have a job with people telling you they are happy in their jobs.

How Do You Measure Up?

During the great recession, organizations pruned back the limbs of their middle management ranks substantially, until there was nothing left but top growth. Many still haven't filled in those areas that were left barren. What will this mean for your company over the next ten years as we see a dramatic shift in workplace demographics?

Take a look at the demographics in your workplace. Are you at risk? By that I mean, do you have a workforce that will topple over the moment you lose some of your older, more experienced people? Are the people in your organization ready to step up the moment they are called to the front lines?

Workforce Planning

Workforce planning is a process used to identify the human capital required to meet the goals of the organization. Included are strategies to meet those requirements. Workforce planning includes identifying:

- the right number of people required based on your strategic plan
- the competencies (knowledge, skills, and abilities) people in the organization will need in order to support the goals of the business
- the positions that will be needed by the organization
- the timing of when people will need to be in place

Workforce plans are similar to insurance plans. They are helpful to have, but few people really want to think about them.

If you are part of a large organization that already has a workforce plan in place, I recommend you occasionally review this plan to make sure it's being adjusted for changes in your business and changes in personnel. If you don't have a plan, then this would be a good time to work with your team to create one. Smaller organizations—especially those with only a few employees—can get away with more informal planning.

Keeping Afloat When Others Are Drowning

As the economy slowly recovers, there appears to be an ample supply of job candidates due to the high rates of unemployment associated with the recession. However, the waters are about to get stormy as the economy moves into full recovery. We'll see a surge of people finding employment, while at the same time older workers will be sailing off into the sunset. How long do you think your company can tread water?

My most successful clients are looking out over the horizon and realizing that if they are going to make it safely to shore, they will have to start swimming now. They are no longer looking at their people as anchors weighing them down. Instead, they are looking at their staff as people on the relay team who, given the right coaching, can outswim the competition.

You can do the same. But you have to be willing to stop thinking of your employees as expenses and begin thinking of them as assets that are as precious as gold. And I don't mean just repeating that throwaway line, "Our people are our most important asset"; I mean demonstrating this attitude day in and day out.

Changes You Will Need to Make to Win the Race for Talent

If you are going to outswim the competition and win this race for talent—particularly millennial talent—you are going to need to throw a recession mentality off the boat. Here's what I mean by this: resist the temptation to "buy" people on sale. Just because you can get a candidate easily doesn't mean you should. There are lots of people who can be bought "on sale" these days as they exhaust financial options. Heck, they'll probably work for free just to get a foot in the door. But that doesn't mean you shouldn't pay good people what they are worth. I'd rather have an employee feel great about his work and treat my customers well than have him question every day how he got himself into this position and, more importantly, how he will get himself out of it.

End the reign of indentured servitude. Employees are tired of carrying the weight of two jobs on their shoulders in the name of team spirit. It's fine to ask people to take on more until you can find the right person to replace the employee who recently left. Just make sure this temporary move doesn't turn into a permanent situation.

A new era is upon us. I call this the era of "fearless flyers." The model that promised, "You'll always have a job as long as you honor the terms of our agreement" was washed away years ago when baby boomers experienced firsthand what it was like to be made redundant by firms like IBM and other blue-chip companies that had once prided themselves on offering people lifelong employment. There is no such thing as employment security anymore, which means that employees are no longer being held back by fear. They've figured out that if they leap they'll be fine, even if they don't soar on their first attempt to leave the nest.

This is particularly true among millennials. Many are still living at home and can take risks without worrying about paying the mortgage. Employers no longer consider job-hopping a negative, so there is no reason to stick around for the sake of your résumé. In fact, working too long for one employer can be viewed as a weak spot on your résumé or the kiss of death. Today's fast-growing companies often seek candidates who can easily adapt to change. A job seeker who has worked for one company over their entire career may find it harder to convince an employer he is nimble and can adapt easily. Candidates who've worked solely for companies like the now defunct Enron know firsthand how difficult it can be to search for work when your only employer is one that most would like to forget.

Employers looking to keep their share of the talent pool will do better by helping their people improve their skills so they can better serve customers rather than worrying about investing in people who may not be around two years down the road. You never know what the future will bring. The people who fly away from your company today could very well be your customers tomorrow. That is, if you treat them well while they are in your employ.

Focus on what's in it for your employees, not what's in it for you. Younger workers are motivated by what's in it for them. They seek employers who will accommodate their schedules and allow them to do work that's interesting to them. Compare that with the old days, when everyone was working together for the good of the company. This dramatic shift requires a new approach to recruitment and retention. Failing to make this shift means you will likely have difficulty finding qualified applicants for positions usually filled by young people.

Rethink your approach to long-term hiring. Employees used to accept job offers thinking they would stay for at least three years or until their stock options fully vested. Many have watched their options go underwater and are no longer willing to hang onto a sinking ship.

In this era of "fearless flyers," I constantly tell my clients that it's important to maximize the talent while they have it, as you can pretty much guarantee that no relationship will last forever. That's why I strongly suggest they always have a plan B—that is, a plan for what they will do when a key hire leaves.

The Game of Life (Version 2.0)

Do you remember Milton Bradley's Game of Life? It was a childhood favorite of mine. When I played the game back in the 1970s, the rules were quite different than they are today. The game came with a board that contained a spinner as well as game pieces. You picked up your car. You added a spouse of the opposite sex, you drove the route without a GPS, and you added the standard two kids to your car. You then continued amassing your fortune as you wove your way toward retirement.

Life today is much different. In fact, you can now play LIFE on your mobile phone and tablet, items that didn't even exist when I was coming of age. The newest version of the Milton Bradley game is appropriately called The Game of Life: ZappED Edition, as zapped is exactly the way many employers feel these days as they try to navigate the 2.0 version of life. Here's how Milton Bradley describes the game today: "You still get to move your car from space to space and select your path to retirement, but now you spin, get paid, sue other players, and make important decisions all on your iPad. Don't want to be just a plain peg? Go ahead and customize your peg character and add a peg-sessory!"

These changes reflect life in the twenty-first century. People no longer feel compelled to take the traditional routes to success. In fact, many skip college altogether. Some never marry while others marry more times than Elizabeth Taylor. Blended families seem more the norm than the exception. People take on spouses of the same sex or life partners who don't fit the traditional mold. Many people choose to be single, and some choose to do so while raising a family.

Here's what you need to know about today's players in the game of life, so you can play to win:

Young People	Mid-Career Employees
• Keep reminding me why I should remain in your employ. • Convince me this work will be worth my time. • Tell me how my work will make the world a better place. • Show me what's in it for me. • What's next? Where am I going from here? • Don't confuse my ability to get work done quickly as laziness. • Offer flexible work schedules. • Provide interesting work. • Offer opportunities for continuous development.	• Demonstrate to me that I'm next in line for a well-deserved promotion. • Allow me to step out and reenter the workplace after raising young children, without a penalty. • Bring back the pay raise—life keeps getting more expensive. • Provide nontraditional benefits for my nontraditional lifestyle. • Show me that I'm valued. • Invest in me—I'm still interested in learning.
Re-Launchers (reentering the workforce)	Off-Rampers (heading toward the retirement exit)
• Understand that my skills are transferrable—I've got more to give than meets the eye. • Realize that I'm reliable and available. • Teach me what I don't know—contrary to what you may have heard, I'm not afraid of technology. • Give me a chance and I'll give you a chance.	• Realize that I'm not leaving anytime soon. • Treat me as though I'm mentally and physically fit for duty—because I am. • Understand that I still have a lot to offer. • Suspend your prejudice about older workers—I do know how to use a computer. • Don't worry that I'm after your job. • Help me to transfer my knowledge to those less experienced.

Of course we understand that, unlike in board games, we cannot simply put people in a box and expect they will fit. These descriptions are meant to catch your attention and to get you to start thinking out of the box.

A Work Environment for the Ages

Global consulting and service firm Deloitte recognized it was losing valuable employees at a point in time when it could least afford the drain. Employees, particularly women, were exiting the firm because they were unable to balance the demands of work and family. The firm knew this issue wasn't going to go away on its own and that immediate action was required. Deloitte began with a commitment to regularly surveying and listening to the voices of employees. The firm made many changes, including the addition of sponsorship programs and the introduction of the Women in Leadership (WIN) program. These programs have contributed to a reduction in employee turnover and a happier workforce. But the firm didn't stop there.

Deloitte also launched the Deloitte University Leadership Center for Inclusion. Deloitte has created a broad definition of inclusion that brings in the Women's Initiative (WIN) and other forms of diversity, as well as addressing generational issues, workplace flexibility, and employee well-being.

Invited to the launch were key stakeholders, employees, a former governor, clients, and thought leaders. I had the privilege of attending this event, where I had the opportunity to sit down with Deborah DeHaas, Deloitte's chief inclusion officer, and Jennifer Steinmann, chief talent officer, to discuss Deloitte's philosophy on engaging employees. "We consider our employees colleagues for life. We stay in close contact both formally and informally with people who are no longer with the firm," said Steinmann. She went on to explain how the firm recognizes that needs change as people move through life. "We have a Personal Pursuits program that allows someone to step away for up to five years. We've had employees take this time to write books, train for the Olympics, and care for a loved one. You bring greater creativity and energy to your work if you explore other areas of your life."

"It was very deliberate that we selected very senior partners for these roles in inclusion leadership. We wanted people who could influence," noted DeHaas. "You can't take your foot off the gas. You have to keep moving forward."

(continues)

Deloitte anticipates that by 2016, gen Y (born in 1982* and thereafter) will make up more than 50 percent of its workforce. This will yet again change the DNA of the organization. Deloitte isn't sitting idle, waiting for this to happen. The company is already working to address changes in the environment to better meet the needs of this new generation.

*There is no consensus over the exact dates of birth for gen Y.

Companies of all sizes should be looking out over the horizon and taking note of the changes that are likely to occur. Making preparations today to address the evolving environment will result in better decisions being made all around.

Five Myths about Today's Workers

Executives and business owners are operating on myths regarding today's workforce that are far from reality. Here are five worth mentioning.

1. **People are lucky to have a job.** If you keep thinking this and treating people as if it's true, then you will be the one looking for a job, as many economies around the world continue to pick up. Are you still betting on the fact that people are lucky to have a job?

2. **Older workers are having a tough time finding work.** This is partially true, but many are doing just fine. Within the last six months, a number of my so-called "older worker" friends have secured new employment. What you may find surprising is that not one of these people was actively looking for work. All were contacted by competitors and plucked right

out of organizations that falsely believed these workers were lucky to have a job.

3. **People will work for peanuts.** How would you feel if you were paid in peanuts instead of company stock? I'm guessing that unless you are an elephant, this idea wouldn't be all that appealing. Yet, employers play the "How low can you go" game with job seekers all the time. Sure, you might get lucky and secure someone who doesn't mind working for peanuts. Of course, that person will stampede out the door (along with the investment you just made in his training) the moment a more fulfilling offer comes along.

4. **If we offer a job, the candidate will take it.** I receive calls just about every week from employers complaining that the job offer they've extended has been turned down. Through further investigation, we find that the candidates had choices. Keep this in mind when interviewing your next round of candidates, as the interviewing process is a two-way street. The candidate has to like you as much as you like the candidate.

5. **I'm your only option.** I've observed job interviews during which the hiring manager has conducted the interview as if this job opportunity were the applicant's only option. But that's not necessarily true these days. The extension of unemployment benefits has given people options. And many are choosing to stay unemployed rather than taking a job that will likely have them back on the street again soon.

Completely eliminate these myths from your belief system, and root them out of your colleagues' beliefs, and you will have taken the first step toward attracting top talent.

Rule of Attraction

Create a workforce plan for your business. Through the planning process you will identify areas where you may be at risk for losing top people, and you can take action to prevent this from happening. You will also be able to determine what you need to do today to prepare your people to take on new roles tomorrow.

The Laws of Attraction

The basic laws of attraction have been around since the days of Adam and Eve. Yet, technology has changed the way attraction plays out. Back in the early days, you were introduced to the person you were going to spend the rest of your life with. In some cultures, this tradition continues. In most Western countries today, however, you rarely hear about couples finding each other the old-fashioned way. Instead, they are using the web to find (and check out) potential mates.

For years, employers depended on an approach to sourcing talent that was similar to old-fashioned dating, whereby introductions were the name of the game. Headhunters would pair those they felt naturally fit together. The "good old boy" system provided opportunities for people in the know to find one another. Offspring could enter organizations through the back door, with a key provided by a parent. The talent pipeline was full.

Until, that is, companies began to sever and destroy their relationships with the people who fed them their best candidates. Some did this by slashing recruitment fees. Others burned bridges by using a machete to reduce their payroll budgets, without giving those being cut any anesthesia. Any love that employees might have felt for their employers quickly dissipated as they witnessed the way their companies handled the reduction of their workforces. Never in a million years did employers think their tactics would become front-page news on people's "personal pages," since these pages weren't in existence when employers began to behave badly.

Much has changed in terms of attracting employees, yet many employers are operating as if things are the same. Employers continue to use recruiting methodologies that are tactical in nature. Job requisitions are filed; standard postings are placed on job boards with the hope that the right people will apply. It certainly could happen, but wouldn't you rather invest your time and resources in an approach that has better odds of success?

The Difference Between Recruitment and Attraction

There is a difference between recruitment and attraction. Recruitment is the process used to find and hire the best-qualified candidate for a job vacancy. The typical candidate recruiting process is geared toward active job seekers and is based on a transactional approach. In larger organizations, the hiring manager sends the requisition to the in-house recruiter who in turn attempts to fill the position as quickly and efficiently as possible . . . with an emphasis on quickly. This form of recruiting is measured with such quantitative metrics as time-to-fill and cost-per-hire. Of course, neither of these metrics actually measures what is most important: the quality of the hire. Traditional recruitment can be effective when companies are reaching out to those who are actively seeking employment. However, passive candidates today (those who aren't actively looking for a new position) are not usually driven by financial needs; they are driven by the desire for growth, meaningful work, challenge, and opportunity.

Attraction happens when an organization has a pull that brings people into its field. Attraction is what gets a passive job seeker to take action: he finds the company and/or the opportunity irresistible.

Why Attraction Trumps Recruitment Every Time

Some companies spend a good chunk of their revenues on advertising and marketing in their attempts to attract people to their brand. Others, like Apple, rely on the community of what I call "Appleangelists" to spread the word for them. You will rarely see an Apple user revert to using a PC. If a person did, she'd no longer be part of the Apple community. Yet we see people defecting from brands all the time when either the advertisements stop or another brand comes along with more boastful advertising.

Companies that are known throughout the employment underground as great places to work have no problems getting attention when they have a position that needs to be filled. Sometimes these businesses will have a particular candidate in mind and will contact this person directly to invite him in for an interview. Rarely are their requests declined. That's because these companies understand that candidates connect with (or choose to disconnect from) a company's brand before they set foot through a company's doors. For most, their minds have been made up long before they've been notified about a job opening.

In situations where a particular candidate hasn't been identified, the employer will put the word out and then brace itself for the influx of qualified candidates expressing an interest in working for the company. This is just one example of the power of magnetism.

A recent LinkedIn survey reported that 83 percent of full-time employees classify themselves as passive job candidates open to taking positions with other organizations if the job was right for them. Eric Pratum was one of these passive candidates:

> I was happy working at a marketing agency that worked only with nonprofits but was approached by the founder of this company with an opportunity to help teens get better grades, prepare for college, find careers they love, and learn life skills often not covered in school. I had no plans to leave my company. The decision ultimately came down to me feeling that I could have a bigger effect on the world if I was helping teens to grow into a better adult life.

Pratum is now the head of marketing for the education start-up Empower.me, which provides online tools to help teens prepare for college and life success.

Better-Quality Candidates at a Lower Cost

Today's candidates are applying for more than a paycheck. The results of a survey conducted by CareerBuilder and Inavero of 4,500 job seekers nationwide found that most considered starting salary less important than the perception of the organization with which they were interviewing. When asked whether they'd take a job for less money at the organization they'd most like to work for, 70 percent said they would accept even if the salary offer were 5 percent less than their lowest acceptable salary. Fifty-eight percent would accept an offer 10 percent less than their salary floor.

Fifty-one percent of job seekers would still take a job at their ideal company for 15 percent less.

There are, of course, considerable ongoing savings that occur when a top candidate accepts a position with your firm and is willing to accept a lower salary because the connection is so strong. I personally felt this way when I accepted the position at my dream employer. As someone who was responsible for establishing pay structures in companies, I had firsthand knowledge that the amount being offered to me was 20 percent below market. But none of that mattered to me. I had experienced what it was like to be paid handsomely while working in a firm where everyone was miserable, including me. My dream employer pulled me in with the promise of a better future, which I had for a number of years.

This doesn't mean that companies who aren't having any problems attracting talent should consider dropping their salaries. Doing so could have a ripple effect throughout the organization. It's also important to recognize that, for many, fair and equitable compensation goes hand in hand with being treated as a valuable partner, instead of just another worker in a sea of cubicles.

When companies are able to pull candidates into their field of attraction, they are able to substantially lower the cost of acquiring top talent. When quality candidates come directly to an organization, the company doesn't have to pay high recruitment fees, which range from 20 to 30 percent of annual compensation. The organization doesn't have to shell out tons of money for advertising on job posting boards, nor does it have to fly all over the country attending career fairs. The prospective employee may not be dismayed when an organization doesn't have the funds to provide a relocation package. Pratum chose to relocate himself and his wife across the country at his own expense in order to work for Empower.me—a substantial savings for the company and a move that Pratum does not regret.

Go Get 'Em!

Talk is great, but at the end of the day, action is what gets the job done. Julie Kahn, senior vice president of Entercom New England, one of the largest broadcast companies in the United States, knows a good salesperson when she sees one. Kahn started her business career in sales and still loves deal making.

Kahn was recently honored with one of the Girl Scouts of Eastern Massachusetts's Leading Women Awards. Prior to the awards breakfast, each honoree is matched up with a Girl Scout who will be presenting the award to her. As luck would have it, Kahn was matched with a Scout who had won awards for selling more boxes of cookies than any other Scout. "When I met this scout, I was blown away by her ability to put together a strategic sales plan that included something that resembled a war map," reminisces Kahn. "She knew exactly where she was going to go to sell cookies and, like a general, she moved forward with confidence. She knew exactly how to market her product. This Scout sold over 5,000 boxes of cookies during one cookie drive."

Knowing that pearls are highly valued by Girl Scouts (Juliette Gordon Low, who founded Girl Scouts in 1912, sold her own pearls to help the organization grow), Kahn decided to purchase pearl earrings for her Scout. At the awards ceremony she told the Scout, "In lieu of a promise ring, this is a promise gift that you will come work for me when you complete your education." I asked Kahn what she would do if this young lady actually contacted her sometime in the future, and she said, "I'd hire her!"

Kahn's approach to hiring is a reminder of how you can find people with high potential in places you'd least expect. Kahn advises executives to seize the opportunity when someone blows you away. She has hired waiters who have treated her with utmost care, as well as retail people who unknowingly demonstrated their ability to upsell her, while leaving her with a good feeling on the way out the door. You'd better hope that some of your top people aren't moonlighting in New England, or you may soon find they are in Kahn's employ.

Mark Triest, president of Ex Libris North America, a global business that is a leading provider of library automation solutions, is another executive who has gone after people vigorously. In a recent conversation, Triest told me how challenging it was to find salespeople with a background in library sciences. At the end of our conversation, he was reminded that he actually knew the people he wanted to have on his team. We had a follow-up conversation a month later, and Triest went from having three sales openings to being fully staffed, without paying any agency fees. I asked him how he managed to do this. He said, "I did what you told me. I went out and got 'em!"

The Power of Speed

As I was writing this book, I received a note from my cousin's wife, whose son was looking at different job opportunities in the restaurant industry. She was thrilled to announce that her son was on his way to California to begin his management training at a fast-growing restaurant chain. She went on to say that he received a call from the company's recruiter within *one minute* of submitting his online application. His background with a top-name restaurant chain must have been quite appealing to a chain that has high hopes of achieving similar, if not higher, levels of success.

Unlike other companies, this one knew what it wanted and chose not to play the "We can't possibly show him how interested we are so we'll let him wait" game. The company went after what it wanted and it got him.

What's the average length of time it takes your business to contact a candidate who has applied for work at your company? If your dream candidate found her way through your portal, could you react as quickly as this company did to let the person know you thought she was something special? Or would your process repel the candidate and allow her to bounce into your competitor's field of attraction?

The Seven Laws of Attraction

Much has changed—and will continue to change—in terms of what today's workforce seeks in an employer. As an employer pursuing top talent, you need to be fully aware of what job seekers are looking for when they are considering potential employers.

As you read through the Seven Laws of Attraction, be sure to ask yourself and those around you how you fare in terms of attraction. Then be prepared to make necessary changes so that you appeal to the candidates you are pursuing.

Law Number One: Beauty Is in the Eye of the Candidate

Have you ever wondered what some people see in their spouses? They see qualities you don't, because beauty is in the eye of the beholder. Luckily, people are attracted to different things, or everyone would be going after one person while the rest of the population stood alone on the sidelines. The same principle holds true with job candidates.

Job seekers from different disciplines define attraction differently. For example, top marketing candidates often look for firms that are a bit off-center. They want to be in an environment where thinking out of the box is encouraged. Compare this with engineers, who typically look for innovative companies where they will have access to the latest in technology.

The problem with most organizations is that they haven't given much thought to whom they are trying to pull in and what would make them appear attractive to these candidates. So they go with a look that they think will appeal to everyone, and they end up appealing to no one. By that I mean that they offer generic benefits, use standard job descriptions, and feature website templates that shout, "We're ordinary!" You'll never attract someone extraordinary with this approach!

Law Number Two: Beauty Comes from Within

Companies invest a great deal of money in marketing to create the illusion they are something they are not. All you have to do is take a stroll down the supermarket aisle and see all the "naturally flavored" products being touted as healthy choices. A team of scientists with no relationship to Mother Nature creates these "naturally flavored" products. Consumers are smartening up to these devious tactics and are changing to products made by those they trust.

Prospective employees are becoming more sophisticated as well. Businesses attempting to woo talent will often present themselves as something they are not. They may try to sell job seekers a bill of goods by telling them they will have total autonomy, when in fact every decision in the company must go through two layers of approvals. Their websites might contain stock photos of diverse personnel, though the majority of employees in the firm represent one race. They may give the illusion they are a hip place to work when they send their youngest staff members to the career fair. But what happens when the candidates are hired and quickly discover that the only hip thing going on in the company is the senior partner's upcoming hip replacement operation?

We call these maneuvers bait and switch. Here's the thing. If you should happen to fool people into taking a job with you by creating a misimpression, it won't be long before they find out the truth. Some may reluctantly stay, joining the ranks of the disengaged, but others will flee, wasting all those recruitment dollars invested in them. If you're lucky, they won't use their social networks to warn others that your company is one that should not be trusted.

Law Number Three: Reputation Matters

Most companies these days will do a Google search on candidates before bringing them in for an interview. This type of due diligence saves hiring managers from wasting valuable time on candidates who don't appear to be right for the job. Today's younger workers are about as transparent as a pair of nylons, and many reveal aspects of their lives for all to see with no regard to how it might impact their employability. For example, photos of the employee winning a Jell-O shot contest might not be the image you want your customers to see should they decide to Google their new pharmaceutical representative—unless, of course, your company sells medication to cure hangovers.

You'd be a fool to think that today's job seekers aren't doing the same thing. Most candidates are checking you out before deciding whether yours is a workplace they'd like to be part of. Brent Rasmussen, president of CareerBuilder North America, was quoted in a CareerBuilder press release as saying, "Workers approach their job search much like a consumer purchase, using multiple avenues to evaluate potential employers months before they take action and apply to positions." Rasmussen added, "It's important for companies to engage candidates at every touch point."

Websites like Glassdoor.com provide an inside look at jobs and companies. Current and former employees are encouraged to post the pros and cons of their workplaces. Here's an example of what a current or former employee might be saying about your company. This comes straight from the pages of Glassdoor.com:

RUN THE OTHER WAY!

Pros—The people at XYZ Company were very nice to work with. The average age of coworkers was probably around 25, so it is easy to form friendships.

Free Wall Street Journals!

Cons—Where to begin . . . [Note: Had I listed every con this person posted, I would have had enough material for another book.]
   Needless to say, very little learning/creative thinking actually took place in this work environment. I felt as if I was killing brain cells every time I entered a number into the computer. The first job that you take should help to develop fundamental skills in the career you choose to pursue. Other than a paycheck, I felt this was a waste of time. The turnover in this department is also exorbitantly high! I think about 30 people left while I was there. Unreal!

Advice to Senior Management—Yes, the point of a business is to generate a profit. However, it is senior management's responsibility to create an environment that is beneficial to employees of the firm. Many people that I have talked to have a bad taste in their mouth from working at XYZ Company. You never know who your next big client may be!

Some of you may be holding your breath, praying this review isn't about your company. The fact that you think it might be says that you have an inkling there is a problem with your company's reputation. Stop worrying and start doing something about it.

You may believe that you don't have to worry about your online reputation because you mostly employ an older workforce. I can tell you from personal experience that people of all ages are still dishing about your company. They may not being doing it online, but they are talking to one another while waiting for their kids to have a turn at bat on the Little League field or when they are passing the dip at the neighborhood potluck dinner. They are also scanning the headlines on their iPads and deciding whether they want to be part of a firm where the CEO has just been accused of sexually harassing one of his employees or using the company jet for personal trips to his vacation home in the Bahamas.

Law Number Four: Looks Matter

I remember growing up and hearing how looks don't really matter and that it's what's inside that really counts. I found this confusing, as the pretty girls were always the most popular girls, and many appeared to have nothing inside. I'm no longer propagating this myth with my own daughter. Instead, I am telling her to put her best foot forward. I would suggest you do the same.

The first thing most job seekers do is go to the company website to check out a business they may be interested in. It's usually a matter of seconds, not minutes, before they decide if they've arrived at a place worth exploring. What do people see when they go to your company website? Do the images align with the message you are trying to convey?

Job seekers at career fairs also have their eyes wide open when it comes to first impressions. Do your recruiters have what they need to present your company in the best light, or are they handing out dated materials that you are trying to use up before investing in more brochures? Looks matter, and if you don't believe this is so, you are only kidding yourself.

Law Number Five: Attraction Must Be Mutual

For many, attraction is about connecting emotionally with someone or something. Starbucks is a great example of a company that fosters such a bond. The company has created a magnetic attraction that is the envy of its competitors, and it has done this by connecting with the hearts and minds of employees and, many would argue, with the wallets of consumers.

I recall a conversation I had with the VP of auxiliary services at a major Boston college. Her responsibilities included staffing the campus coffee shops, and she shared with me her difficulties recruiting students to work at the campus Dunkin' Donuts. She was puzzled by the fact that she had no problems hiring people to work at the campus Starbucks. She quickly learned that perception is everything. It's seen as cool to work as a barista at Starbucks, yet it's not cool to work at Dunkin' Donuts. Starbucks has done an exceptional job of making this brand distinction among those who are behind the counter serving cups of joe or, in this case, caffé latte.

Starbucks employees represent the brand. The company knows the type of people it must hire in order to connect with its customers, and it has no problem courting workers to take entry-level jobs. Can your company say the same? Are you seeking to attract those who would find you attractive? Or are you looking for employees who are currently way out of your league?

Law Number Six: The Powerful Attraction of a Great Boss

Have you ever noticed how some bosses bring along teams filled with star players when they join a new organization, while others struggle to hold onto the talent they've hired? Great bosses are a precious resource. Luckily for you, they can be cultivated. That is, if you are willing to rid your organization of those not-so-great bosses and make the necessary investments to help managers become the type of boss everyone would love to have. Take a close look at bosses who have a following. What is it about these people that others find so compelling? You'll most likely find that they give credit where due, they recognize people for their contributions, and they go to the mat for their employees when other leaders might back off.

Take the following challenge. In thirty seconds, list the names of all the great bosses in your organization. If you can't think of any, then we need to talk.

Law Number Seven: Fatal Attraction Can Be Fatal

Just because you have people stalking your company in the hope of being hired doesn't mean that you are doing a great job of attracting talent to your organization. Having the wrong people applying for work with your company will do nothing but clog up your talent pipeline. You'll spend hours combing through résumés in search of the right people, even as the right people are obtaining interviews elsewhere. By the time you finally sift through the pile, the talent you desire may no longer be on the market.

If you find that you are attracting professional job seekers (those who have made a full-time job out of looking for work), then a new approach may be in order, one that will yield you a select group of candidates who embody exactly what you are looking for.

Rule of Attraction

Take a look at your recruitment strategy. Are you recruiting people, or are you attracting them? If attraction isn't part of your recruitment strategy, then it's time to reboot your talent acquisition and retention strategy and bring it into the twenty-first century.

4

Creating a Workplace Where Employees Are Evangelists

All these theories about the power of magnetic workplaces are just that if you don't do anything to create this type of energy in your own organization. Think about the types of companies you most enjoy doing business with. These are the companies you would continue to patronize even if you could find the product for a lower price or the service for a lower fee.

For a long time, I was enamored with Dell computers. There were certainly other computers out there that could get the job done for a lot less. Yet I continued to order my computers through Dell because I thought the company had cutting-edge products and great customer service. Until a new Apple Store opened in my area. Coincidentally, the store opened just as my computer began to crash on what seemed like a daily basis.

Every time I walked by the Apple Store in the mall, I felt the energy radiating from inside. I couldn't help but notice the laughter and the smiling faces of both employees and customers. And then it happened. I decided that I was tired of trying to recover data that mysteriously disappeared from my PC. My tech guy and I were on a first-name basis, and I knew more about his personal life than that of my friends because of the increasing amount of time we were spending together.

I decided I deserved better. I was tired of looking into that store from the outside, and so I took the plunge. I ordered my first Mac and I never looked back. A funny thing happened when I decided to give my business to a company where employees love to work and customers love to do business. I stopped doing business with other companies that clearly didn't value my business and sought out those where I was welcome. The differentiating factor in almost all these companies is the people and their ability to treat me like an individual rather than one of the masses.

Common Traits of Exceptional Workplaces

In my consulting practice, I've worked with some extraordinary companies, including Best Buy, Keurig, and The Boston Beer Company. These businesses don't rest on their laurels. They understand that creating a customer-centric culture is the beginning rather than the end, as cultures must be fed in order to be sustained.

Following are the top ten traits common to exceptional workplaces:

1. Employees Feel Empowered

Employees can make decisions on the spot to correct problems without going to their managers for approval. They can do so without worrying that their managers will take them to task when they find out what the employee has done on behalf of the customer. The Ritz-Carlton is the gold standard for empowering employees. One of the hotel company's remarkable policies permits employees to spend up to $2,000 making any single guest satisfied.

Those of you who are small business owners may be thinking, "I'll go bankrupt if I allow my employees to spend freely." But you don't have to have a Ritz-Carlton budget to empower your people. Here's an example. I had lunch the other day at a small creperie. My daughter ordered the ala carte crepe and requested steak and cheese. What she got instead was steak, onion, peppers, and cheese. Not exactly what was described on the menu. We returned the crepe and changed the order when we were told that the steak had been precooked with onions and peppers. The server delivered the new crepe to the table along with an apology and a $5 gift certificate. We left feeling full and satisfied and will certainly return to this establishment.

Imagine this server's frustration if she had to go to her boss every time and ask for permission to spend $5 to delight a customer. I suspect that after a while she would feel like a kid asking a parent for her weekly allowance.

Empowerment in exceptional companies goes beyond giving employees the ability to fix problems. People who feel empowered speak up when they have ideas they believe should be considered. They do so without concern for the chain of command. These are the people who will warn you that you are about to make a costly mistake because they don't fear retribution if they happen to be wrong.

2. Sense of Purpose

Have you ever worked in an organization where you had no sense of purpose? By that I mean you had no idea why you were there and whether anyone would notice if you decided one day not to show up. I have. In my situation, I knew I was there for one thing—to make the owner wealthier. But that wasn't enough to sustain my level of commitment. In fact, the harder I worked and the wealthier he got, the more dissatisfied I became. It wasn't long before I was taking my unhappiness out on those I was serving. My sense of purpose was nowhere to be found, and my values did not align with those of the organization. The results were disastrous for all parties involved.

Magnetic Leader Jimmy St. Louis

You cannot have passion for the work you do without a sense of purpose and alignment with the core values of the company you are working for.

Former NFL player Jimmy St. Louis, CEO of Advanced Healthcare Partners, a leading health-care management and consulting company based in Tampa Bay, Florida, has experience competing both on and off the field. St. Louis knows the importance of having all players on his team heading in the same direction. He also believes in the need to keep things simple. He must be doing something right, because his company is experiencing a high velocity of growth.

"Changing the business of healthcare." That's Advanced Healthcare Partners' vision, and St. Louis isn't afraid to drop clients who don't align with what his company is trying to do.

St. Louis asserts:

"We kept the process simple when establishing our core values. We asked ourselves the following:

What are we about?

What is the goal of the company?

What are we trying to accomplish?

What do we want to live by on a daily basis?"

(continues)

After answering these questions, Advanced Healthcare came up with the following guiding principles:

Our Mission

To create a new standard of healthcare by providing our partners with a strategic business platform that will deliver the highest level of quality care for customers and patients.

Our Vision

To change the business of healthcare.

Our Value

Be fun to be around—we truly value our partnership and enjoy what we do. Our team is energetic, motivated, and results oriented.

Give back—we are committed to the community. All of the AHP teammates hold community board positions, and we continuously give back to various causes in all of our communities.

Add value . . . always—we are committed to always adding value. If AHP cannot add value, we know that is not the right partnership.

Always push the status quo—we are committed to pushing the status quo and never accepting no for an answer. Our progressive thinking and nature is what drives our mission and the success of our partners.

Be selective—AHP is focused on working with clients in specific niches of the healthcare industry and is committed to finding only the right partners that can benefit from one another.

Simplicity: it's a word St. Louis uses often. Simple. Yet it really works.

A sense of purpose comes with an understanding of how you fit into the big picture. Knowing exactly what your job is and why it's important that you perform it well is part of the recipe. As CEO or other senior executive, it's your job to make sure you hire people who are interested in more than just a job. Be sure they desire a sense of purpose. Follow up by communicating why your people matter to you.

3. High Levels of Trust

High levels of trust in an organization create an environment in which people are willing to go above and beyond the call of duty. This type of effort among employees occurs because they don't want to disappoint those who believe in them.

What exactly does a trusting organization look like? It's actually more of a feel than a look. Employees sense that the boss isn't standing over their shoulder waiting for them to fail. The professional staff isn't clocking in or out because time spent in the office isn't what's rewarded. Results are all that matter. Leaders are transparent. They don't have hidden agendas nor do they dodge difficult questions.

In a trusting organization, employees are given responsibility for projects that have a direct impact on the success of the organization because leaders trust them. No one questions when they leave the office with a packed briefcase, nor are they asked to leave their cell phones at the front desk because the company is paranoid that its workers might leak photos of its new product.

Here's what trust isn't. It's requiring that your retail employees carry transparent purses for fear that one person may attempt to shoplift a tube of mascara. It's having cameras set up throughout your operation so you can see every move your people make. It's installing an intercom in the kitchen so you can listen in on what your people are saying while they are on break. It's requiring all employees to open up their purses and briefcases on the way out of your workplace to prove they haven't stolen the kitchen sink.

Consumers do business with companies they trust. So do top performers. These people operate best when they feel management is totally honest with them. Trust me when I tell you that great workplaces and outstanding customer experiences are all about trust. When it comes to trust, how does your company rate? What can you do today to build or sustain trust in your organization?

4. Clarity

Organizational clarity is one of those things that many businesses strive for but few attain. Here's why. Companies say they want to achieve top-performing status, yet many either don't know how to get out of their own way or they aren't willing to do the work necessary to make this happen. This is especially true of start-up companies, which, like certain unemployed actors, believe it's only a matter of time before they will be discovered. Or, in the start-up's case, acquired for obscene amounts of money. If you've ever working in a start-up, you know exactly what I mean, as there is often confusion over who is in charge, what the priorities are, and even who to turn to with questions.

Here's how you lift the fog and gain clarity in your organization. Invest the necessary time to clearly define your mission, vision, and organizational goals.

This information should then be communicated to employees more than once a year.

Clearly define the roles in the company as well as the reporting structure. Companies usually document this information by creating job descriptions, which adds clarity by defining success as it relates to a specific job. Entrepreneurs tend to shy away from job descriptions because they believe they are too limiting. This concern can be overcome by adding "Other duties as assigned" to every job description.

Next, be sure to document systems and processes. This will significantly reduce confusion and increase clarity. Review your documentation on a regular basis and adjust when necessary.

Clarity allows employees to do their jobs better and faster. Now can you see why clarity is so highly valued?

5. Interesting and Challenging Work

Like many of you, I worked some pretty boring jobs on my way up the corporate ladder. One in particular stands out in my mind. For about a year, I was employed as a file clerk in a small law firm. My job required me to spend hours every day slotting papers and legal documents into the office files. Mind you, this was way before the invention of iPods, so I was forced to do this in total silence. I'd like to think I did a stellar job, but in retrospect, I probably did an average job at best. In fact, I bet those attorneys are still looking for some of the papers I may have misfiled.

Most people seek opportunities in organizations where the work will be interesting and challenging. When they are fortunate enough to find an opportunity that fits the bill, they are usually committed to doing a great job. Anyone who has ever shopped in a big box store knows that there is a direct correlation between an employee's commitment to his job, his satisfaction level, and customer service. We've all experienced what it's like to be rung up by a cashier who'd rather be anyplace but work and makes no effort to hide this fact. Most of us have also experienced what it's like when an employee loves his work and shows it. In fact, this employee may be you.

6. Recognition and Reward for Effort

It's human nature to continue certain behaviors when we are rewarded and recognized. It's also natural to stop doing things when we realize recognition and rewards are not coming our way.

Employees are willing to overlook a lot of things, including used office furniture and lower wages, when they are recognized for their contributions. Employee rewards and recognition can be powerful tools to reinforce behavior that is aligned with the company's mission and goals. They also go a long way in retaining good talent and, in turn, improving the overall customer service experience.

Here are some ideas for showing your employees they are highly valued.

Do something memorable. Take the time to get to know your people, so they are more than just an employee number. This will allow you to reward your employees with something memorable.

It's been almost twenty years since I was called into the CEO's office for what I thought was a routine meeting. Our time together was anything but routine. Rather than discussing another project that he wanted me to do, he told me how pleased he was with my work. He then handed me an envelope. Inside were two tickets to a sold-out Phil Collins concert. You see, in passing I had happened to mention to the CEO my disappointment in being unable to secure tickets to this hot show. I had no idea he was actually listening, as he had a tendency to change subjects rather rapidly. Rather than reward me with a small check for a job well done, he gave me something that I could not get elsewhere. He increased the pull he had on me with just one envelope. Memorable indeed. I hope you will think of this story the next time you want to demonstrate to someone that she is highly valued. Resist the temptation to take the easy way out and instead go out of your way and do something magnetic!

Grant a few hours off. Imagine what it would feel like to have your boss call you into her office and insist that you take the rest of the day for yourself. Can't imagine it? That's because this expression of appreciation is one that is rarely used. However, it's certainly a powerful gesture. It sends the message to the employee that you recognize she is deserving of some time for herself. It's a small gesture that delivers lots of happy memories for those who have experienced it.

Small gestures go a long way. The CEO of LinkedIn recently expressed his love for all his employees by giving each one an iPad Mini of their own. "Jeff 'Winfrey' Weiner decided to give every [LinkedIn] employee an iPad Mini today as a special reward for our recent results," Mike Grishaver, a product manager who works on the company's marketing solutions team, posted on the business social network. Needless to say, the story went viral. Employee enthusiasm trickled over to Twitter, where some wasted no time in tweeting about their new toys. LinkedIn quickly became the object of every employee's affection. Not to mention all the love that overflowed into the PR world. You can certainly adjust this gesture to any budget. You may not have the funds to give everyone a grand gift, but you could consider a meaningful gesture on a smaller scale.

7. Respect

Many of the leaders I meet appear to be too busy to treat people respectfully. Instead, they bark orders as they fly off to their next appointment or they berate employees in front of customers. Then they wonder why these same employees yell at their own people in front of clients.

What's the point of going to work every day if you don't feel respected? Top performers have choices. If you are not going to respect them in the morning (or all day, for that matter), they'll find someone who will.

Regardless of position, treat people the way you'd like them to treat you or your daughter or son. Mind your manners, and don't be surprised when those around you behave the same way. Confront those in your organization who treat people disrespectfully and, if need be, show them the door.

8. Communication Flowing Freely in Both Directions

I've worked in organizations that would make the CIA look like an open book. Closed-door meetings, hushed conversations, and notes slipped into special folders were all part of a day's work. It didn't take long for me to realize I wasn't privy to the information I needed to do my job effectively. I tired after a while and found a place where communication flowed freely through the veins of the organization. I called that place home for quite some time.

Communication jams often occur in the middle of organizations. Somewhere in the communication process, someone fails or forgets to share the information that people need to do their jobs. Consider starting a blog—there are no filters or clogs in this communication system. This will guarantee that your people get to hear firsthand what you are thinking and why you are making certain decisions.

Communication from the bottom to the top often stalls in the middle as well, as too many managers are protecting themselves, playing the game of CYA instead of coming clean and working with senior leaders to fix problems. Make it a point to be visible in the organization. Stopping by an employee's desk to ask how she is doing and sticking around long enough to hear her answer will go a long way to ensure you have all the data you need to run your business effectively.

9. Great Managers

In my consulting practice, I've watched some great managers take great employees with them wherever they go. I don't mean that they necessarily solicit these people from their former employees. They don't have to because their employees know how rare it is to have a great manager. They don't wait for the call. Instead, they call their former bosses and ask, "Hey, got anything for me over there?"

We already touched upon a few positive attributes of great bosses in the Seven Laws of Attraction; below is a more expansive list of what great leaders have in common. Great leaders:

- are great listeners
- put the needs of their employees first
- mentor, support, and champion their people
- reward their people for a job well done, giving credit where credit is due
- help their people gain the skills they need to be promotable
- have their employees' backs

Now tell me, if you had a boss like that, would you ever leave?

10. Strong Leadership

As of this writing, we are in a bit of a stormy economy, although the skies certainly appear to be clearing, at least in certain sectors. One day, business indicators are up and the next day, things are trending downward. Companies with strong leadership are weathering the economy better than those with weak leadership. Employees are choosing to hang on instead of jumping ship.

Customers are still making major purchases but are more cautious in their spending. Most will think twice about doing business with a firm if they know that people inside the company are expressing doubt about the organization's leadership and long-term viability.

People with strong leadership skills have the ability to get things done and attract those with a similar can-do attitude. If you have to ask yourself how strong your leadership team is, then I think you already know the answer: not strong enough. Identify the managers who could benefit from working with a coach and make it a priority to get them the help they need. The sooner, the better.

Employee Engagement and Customer Stickiness

As a business leader who may be spending more time focusing on the numbers than on the people side of the business, you may forget that customers don't do business with companies—they do business with people. You can't force people to be innovators, nor can you push them into providing a great customer experience. It's your job to create an environment that encourages your employees to deliver on your brand's promise. You have to personally select an incredible team who will in turn select other high-caliber people. You have to nurture this team and consistently demonstrate and reward the behaviors you seek in your people.

The Values Institute at DGWB, a Santa Ana, Calif.-based think tank, and *Entrepreneur* magazine recently released a study that explored the reasons some brands stay on top. According to the survey results, today's most

trustworthy brands have created relationships with consumers through experiences that trigger a visceral response.
A strong relationship with consumers is powerful and it
works. When you have it, you have a much stronger affin-
ity, a much stronger business, much stronger growth, and
much stronger results.

You don't have to be a big, name-brand company to
apply this philosophy to your business. When I got married,
it took my husband, who is now a retired dentist, more than
a year to convince me to leave the dental practice where I
had been a patient for quite a long time. I loved everything
about my dentist's office. Most importantly, I had a great
relationship with my hygienist. I probably would have followed her to the other side of the country. Eventually, my
husband wooed me away, and I was thrilled to find that his
staff had a connection to their patients that equaled the
practice I had left. But I have to admit, I did leave kicking
and screaming.

When it comes down to it, customer attraction and loyalty, which in turn lead to growth and increased profitability, boil down to these nine factors:

1. Relationships—the connection a customer has with
    those who represent the company.

2. Kept promises—the ability of your firm to deliver on
    what is promised.

3. Quality—dependable products and services.

4. Innovation—a changing selection of new and better
    products and services.

5. Value—the sense that people are getting their mon-
    ey's worth.

6. Excellent customer service—an assurance that if
    something goes wrong, you will quickly resolve cus-
    tomers' issues.

7. Consistency—a reliable customer experience.

8. Customizable solutions—problem solving tailored to meet clients' specific needs.

9. Ease of access—a simple and seamless process for purchasing products and services.

Five Myths That Stop You from Taking Action

I've come across all sorts of myth-spinning about why a company can't (or shall we say *won't*) become the type of workplace that attracts the best and the brightest. Here are a few of the most common:

1. **It takes a wad of cash to attract top talent.** Studies have shown time after time that money is not usually the deciding factor when candidates are assessing job opportunities. Nowadays, there's no excuse for having a website that doesn't represent your company well, as the cost of creating a stellar site has come down considerably.

2. **We don't have the time or resources.** That's probably because you are spending all your time and money on employee churn. What if, instead, you committed those resources to doing things right the first time around?

3. **It's an employer's market, so we don't need to make the effort.** For some companies, that may indeed be true. But for how long? What will you do when the tables are turned and the people who leave are those you can least afford to lose?

4. **We're really not that special.** Well, if that's how you really feel about your company, then you are right. You should do nothing.

5. **We're so great that everyone knows about us.**
   That might be true today, but with so much competition in the marketplace, will that be true tomorrow?

Rule of Attraction

Define your organization's sense of purpose. Take a page out of Jimmy St. Louis's playbook and ask yourself the following:

What are we about?

What is the goal of the company?

What are we trying to accomplish?

What principles do we want to live by on a daily basis?

Remember to keep it simple.

CHAPTER

Creating a Magnetic Employment Brand

One of my all-time favorite movies is *Field of Dreams*, starring Kevin Costner. The most memorable line from that movie occurs when Costner, who plays an Iowa corn farmer, hears a voice telling him, "If you build it, he will come." I think that mantra must have gotten permanently stuck in the memory banks of a lot of executives, as many of them believe this is all they need to attract an employee or a customer to their business. But "building it" is just half the story. You can wait for a sequel to learn more or you can read on.

You may indeed be the best or most innovative employer around, but what does it matter if no one but you knows it? There are a lot of great businesses in my part of the country that take much longer than is necessary to fill positions with good people. And I happen to live in an area with an abundance of talent looking for work. How can this be? It's because no one knows about these companies, and it takes a long time for them to convince people they really are as good as they say. Think about how much time and money you could save if candidates came to you already convinced that you are the company for them.

Brands, especially employment brands, are about perception. People are attracted by a compelling promise. Brands allow us to circumvent the deep thinking that's associated with decision making to get to the heart of the matter. Do we feel a connection to what's being offered or not?

A recent study published in the *Harvard Business Review*, called "Winning the Race for Talent in Emerging Markets," clarified the key elements that top candidates examine when assessing employers. Workplace attraction is based upon the following:

1. **Company's brand (who we are).** Does our company have a reputation for excellence that may lead to personal advancement?

2. **Purpose (what we do and what we are going to do).** Does the company have a mission and values that are meaningful to potential new hires?

3. **Opportunity (what we offer).** Does the company provide an appealing package to employees (challenging work, training, and intrinsically motivating rewards)?

Let's take as an example one of the world's best-known brands, Google. In a recent survey conducted by Universum, a global organization that builds brands to capture talent, Google is listed as the world's most attractive employer. The survey was based on the preferences of more than 144,000 career seekers with a business or engineering background, from the world's twelve greatest economies. It should come as no surprise that Google tops the global talent attraction index of "The World's Most Attractive Employers 2012," as this company is the whole deal, and is often cited as the gold standard for recruiting and retaining top talent.

In fact, this is a company that never rests on its laurels. Google recently introduced a new employee benefit that lasts into the afterlife. In the event of an employee's death, Google now provides the surviving spouse or domestic partner 50 percent of that person's salary for a decade. The surviving partner will also get all stocks vested immediately. This benefit comes with a "no tenure" requirement, but it covers only U.S. employees right now. And if that wasn't enough, get this: children of the deceased employee will get $1,000 a month from the company until they turn nineteen (or until age twenty-three if they are full-time students). I'm sure you'd agree that this is one company that has no problem filling its talent pipeline.

I recently reconnected with a former client who is now with Google. In fact, he wasn't really looking for a job when Google offered him one but found the attraction impossible to deny. He now spends his days at Google and crosses the country to visit his wife, who still lives on the East Coast. He tells me that what you read and see in the media reflects what life is really like there—strong leadership, incredible benefits, and a great work environment. I know of others with family and friends at Google, and they say the same thing.

You don't have to be in a sexy industry like technology to be considered a catch. Take Trader Joe's, a self-described unique grocery store owned by the Albrecht family, who reside in Germany. This is one retailer that has the ability to be as choosey about its team members as it is about the vendors the company does business with. Why? Because Trader Joe's has created a culture where it's hip to be part of the crew, which is what team members are called. People of all ages are proudly wearing the Trader Joe's Hawaiian shirts as if they were badges of honor.

Trader Joe's has created a magnetic employment brand that attracts like-minded people to the organization. People line up outside the doors for a chance to be a part of something big. A typical Trader Joe's store opening can attract

500 well-qualified people to choose from on the first day of hiring. How many other retailers can boast that type of result? What's more, the lines of prospective employees produce headlines in local papers that result in free advertising for the company.

Granted, not everyone wants to attract, nor should be attracting, hundreds of candidates for each job opening. But surely you'd agree it would be nice to have at least a handful of top people to choose from whenever a position opens up in your firm.

A Lesson from a Lesser-Known Company

Charleston, South Carolina–based SPARC may not be a household name in your part of the world, but this small, fast-growing company (it's grown from five employees to more than two hundred in less than three years' time) has people flying in from all over to tour and experience its business. SPARC, a software development company, has worked diligently to create the type of culture that attracts top talent, including IT people—a scarce commodity, particularly in South Carolina. Perhaps that's because CTO and Chief Evangelist John Smith (team members get to pick their own titles) doesn't view employees as a commodity. He views every hire as a vital member of the team.

Smith notes that most organizations are being run like manufacturing companies, where optimization used to be key. "Today, what we do is innovation. If you are using the same culture to drive innovation that you used to drive optimization, then you are probably getting one-tenth of what you could be getting in terms of results and customer attraction."

SPARC is a culture-led organization, and that magnetism can be felt from lands far away. "We've never paid anyone's relocation here. Our brand and our culture help us pull people in," notes Smith.

(continues)

Smith believes that we all have one life, and he has incorporated this into everything the company does. "You should take your work life home and your home life to work. It should be accepted in both places," states Smith. At SPARC, employees are required to work from home one day a month. They have unlimited vacation time and are encouraged to invite their kids to work. Dogs are welcome as well.

Unique aspects of life at SPARC include:

- Co-leads that share responsibility
- Company-wide involvement in the hiring process (anyone can veto a potential hire)
- A measurement for civility at work
- Senior leaders without desks; most move around
- Requests that employees complain about something, which allows the company to fix problems before it's too late

Everything SPARC does can be done by your firm. "I'm on a mission to prove to the world that work doesn't have to suck," acknowledges Smith. If you'd care to join him, he'd welcome a visit from you.

Why Being an "Employer of Choice" May Not Be So Great

Before we go further, let's talk about this whole business of being an "employer of choice." You'll never be an employer of choice if you try to be everything to everyone. Think about it: brands that try to attract everyone usually fail. Why? Because they confuse people and wind up attracting no one. Even some of the world's most famous brands have learned the hard way that trying to be everything to everyone simply doesn't work.

Do you remember McPizza? Probably not. That's because McDonald's failed miserably in the mid-nineties when it tried to grab a slice of the pizza market. Aside from the fact that the product was bland, pizza aficionados couldn't stomach the idea of abandoning their favorite pizza joint for a hamburger place trying to also be a pizzeria.

If you are working to create an employment brand that attracts a specific type of candidate, then you should purposely exclude some folks. Here's what I mean. You don't see McDonald's working hard to pull in vegetarians, do you? The company is smart enough to know that its marketing dollars are best spent on grabbing the lion's share of the target market, which is families with young children and meat-eating adults and teens looking for a quick meal.

We can learn a lot about employment branding by examining what marketing gurus do to successfully brand their produces and services. As an employer, you can use this information to create an employment brand that pulls the people you desire toward you. Here's how you really attract the right people to your organization.

Be authentic. Spending your efforts on attracting Ivy League–educated employees to your firm is a complete waste of time and energy for both you and the candidates if what you need are people to do low-level work. Be who you are, and look to attract people who will fit easily into your organization.

Aim your arrow toward one target. If you've ever done archery, you know the goal is to get your arrow to hit the bull's eye. You also know this is unlikely to happen if you are shooting at a bunch of targets in an attempt to get the darn arrow to hit someplace! Yet this is what many companies do when they attempt to pull workers into their organizations. They take a scattered approach to recruiting with the hope that they'll nab the person they truly want. Of course, this takes a tremendous amount of time and requires a lot of additional resources, when all that is needed is one arrow going in the right direction.

Determine who your ideal candidate is and then work backward. Figure out what needs to be done in order to make your workplace attractive to the exact people you are trying to hire. Then take your best shot.

Be bold. The only way to stick out in the crowd is to be different. Every company says it's a great place to work. If this were really true, all companies would have low employee turnover. Put your stake in the ground and tell people what's unique about your organization. Perhaps it's the fact that you prepare your people to run their own businesses. Or maybe you've been able to boil down all those fancy organizational development buzzwords to get at the heart of your company's mission, like Nestlé, whose short and sweet value proposition is "Real People. Real Possibilities." Real good, huh?

Employment Brand Defined

All companies have an employment brand, although many either don't know they have one or wish the one they had could be traded for someone else's. An employment brand is the way you are perceived by prospective candidates and by current and past employees. For example, when you think of UPS, you think of a logistics company that manages to get those Amazon deliveries dropped off at your door. UPS has worked diligently to build a culture in which employees feel cared for and, in turn, the employees care for the company's customers.

I've personally experienced what it's like to try to hire the same type of people that UPS was looking to hire when I worked as director of Human Resources for a company in the overnight delivery business. Given the choice, candidates went with the name brand, and I was left with the UPS rejects.

In recent years, the concept of employment branding has become one of the leading strategies in talent acquisition and retention because employers see it as one of the few long-term solutions to a tightening labor market. The benefit of having a strong employment brand is similar to the power of brands on the product and service side of business. Once your employment brand is well established, candidates, like consumers, will choose you instead of your competitors.

In a recent article in the *Wall Street Journal*, it was noted that, for many companies, employer branding has become a critical management tool, as the emergence of China, India, and Brazil as economic powers and the aging workforces in the United States, European Union, and Japan have increased the competition for skilled workers. More recently, the economic slowdown—and the pressure to cut costs and increase productivity—has made the need to get the best people in the right jobs even more crucial.

The use of employment branding as a strategy to attract talent isn't exclusive to larger employers. In fact, the less well known you are, the more important it is as a strategy. I've worked with businesses of all sizes on their employment brands and have measured the return on investment (ROI). In a short period of time, we have leveraged companies' employment brands so they shift from being a recruitment cost to a being strategic driver of profit. You can do the same.

Establishing a Strong Employment Brand

You have to have a clear sense of the type of talent you are trying to attract to your company, what these people are most interested in, and what you have to offer before you can work on branding your organization. You should be able to come up with a solid employment brand in less than a day by asking yourself the following questions:

1. **What is it about our organization that is attractive to others?** Simply put, why do people choose to work here and why do they stay?

2. **What is our unique value proposition?** A value proposition is a statement of why the total work experience in your organization is superior to that at other companies. It is the reason that people choose to commit themselves to your organization. Here is an example of what I mean: I recently worked with a client, UM International, LLC, that is taking the motorcycle industry by storm. This company is fast becoming known in global markets for its innovation and attention to safety. My client seeks workers who value innovation, so here's the unique value proposition we came up with to attract like-minded people to the organization: "Some companies dream of changing the world. Our company does so one motorcycle at a time." What's your unique value proposition?

3. **What attracted our best talent to our organization and what keeps them here?** The emphasis is on *best* here, as it's really not important why mediocre employees remain in your employ. That's a whole other book.

4. **What's the culture truly like in our company?** I'm not talking about the line you have printed in your recruiting brochure. How would those employed by your firm describe the work environment? Would they say it's intense yet rewarding? Creative? Innovative? Is it a relaxed culture, where people still get things done? Jot down the first words that come to your employees' minds when you ask them to describe your company's

corporate culture, and resist the temptation to filter their words. That will give you a fairly good idea of how to accurately describe your culture to potential candidates. A word of caution: if you don't like what you're hearing, step back and figure out what can be done to shift the culture. Then do this exercise again.

5. **What do your people most value about their employment experience with your firm?** Is it their ability to constantly learn new things? Workplace flexibility? International assignments? That you allow them to bring their pets to work? The more exceptional the answers, the easier it will be to differentiate yourself from the pack.

6. **How would people outside the firm describe your employees?** Ask customers and vendors to briefly describe what comes to mind when they interact with your employees. Do they think your people are the best in the business? A fantastic team with lots of integrity? This will give you an outside perspective on how others see your workplace. Don't be afraid to be shameless here. If you are running a marketing firm and your clients tell you that their revenues have grown exponentially because your people keep delivering the unexpected, then run with that. Remember, your intent is to pull in great people who are attracted to working with other amazing employees. This is certainly not the time to be humble. Use the best of what your clients give you.

7. **What is it about our employees we are most proud of?** Your answers may be work related or they may not be. Perhaps you are most proud of the fact that 75 percent of your employees volunteer in their communities. Or perhaps you have some extremely bright employees on staff who hold patents. Don't be

discouraged if you can't answer this question right away. Spend some time getting to know your employees, and the answers will most likely be in front of you.

8. **What traits do we look for when hiring top talent for our company?** What are the absolute must-haves when we bring new people into our organization? For example, if you work in a CPA firm, chances are you are seeking people who are extremely detailed oriented. If you are running a marketing firm, you are most likely looking for someone with an ability to think outside the box.

9. **What do we offer in terms of benefits to our employees?** Again, the more unique, the better. My motorcycle client offers all employees the opportunity to purchase motorcycles at cost, and also provides motorcycle riding lessons and safety classes for interested employees. Did I mention that, as a group, employees were planning to take occasional afternoons off to ride together into the sunset? Other organizations, like SAS, the world's largest independent analytics business, have an on-site hair and nail salon, which is open to both employees and retirees. Maybe you don't have enough employees to support a full-time nail technician, but this doesn't mean you can't bring someone in-house once a week or give away gift certificates to the local salon and tout this as a benefit.

Creating Your Brand: A Brand Is More Than a Tagline

We've all experienced what it's like to purchase a product or service based on a tagline, only to be disappointed when it doesn't live up to its advertised potential. The same thing happens in businesses when an employment brand doesn't match the reality of the workplace. While words like "transparent" and "entrepreneurial" are lovely descriptors, can you say they accurately reflect the culture of the large financial institution you are managing? The brand communication cannot stray too far from the perceived reality of the brand, or it will feel inauthentic or, worse, set up expectations that cannot be delivered. Don't believe me? Just ask some top people who've recently left your firm what they meant when they said they were leaving for a better opportunity.

Take a look at your answers to the nine questions above, and you will certainly see a pattern. If, by chance, these descriptors are not even close to where you believe your company should be in terms of culture, then you have work to do on the environment before you are ready to devote additional resources to employment branding. Stop reading, bookmark this chapter, and return once you have done the necessary work to create the type of culture that you will be happy leaving as your legacy.

Image Is Everything

In this day and age of multimedia and HD television, everything is magnified. I'm constantly amazed at the crispness of what I see on the screen in front of me. I'm also thankful that I don't have to appear on camera every day and worry about whether my smile lines will be showing. A company announces a layoff, and within minutes a remote camera crew is en route to capture the story. Anything that happens in your company is quickly amplified, as employees tweet and share their work lives with thousands of their so-called friends and LinkedIn connections across the globe.

The Trials and Tribulations of Social Media

Recently, an employee (or shall I say former employee) of HMV, the beleaguered British entertainment retailer, took to Twitter to give the world a play-by-play description of what was going on inside the company as it laid off 190 employees. This employee, who had been an HMV community manager and thus had access to the corporate Twitter account, started live tweeting about the layoffs.

You can imagine the buzz that shot around the globe as a result of one person, an employee the company most likely never thought would be a threat. Now, imagine what will happen if this company rises from the ashes and begins to hire again. The damage has been done, and, thanks to technology, HMV will always be known as the company whose layoff was broadcast live for all to see. Most likely the company will have a difficult time attracting top talent when and if it goes into hiring mode again.

As the CEO, senior executive, or business owner, you are ultimately responsible to manage the company's image. Zappos CEO Tony Hsieh has done an outstanding job of making sure everyone is aware of what's going on inside Zappos. One of the core values of the company is open and honest communication. Hsieh takes the term "open" to a whole new level. Zappos's all-hands-on employee meetings are streamed live on the Internet so that outsiders can see into the workings of the organization. Compare that with the communications of most organizations, which leave both shareholders and potential job seekers wondering if what they are being told is really what is going on inside the organization.

You have the power to manage your company's culture, since culture starts at the top. You are also the one who can share your thoughts on the workplace through your Twitter feed, your LinkedIn page, or a blog for all to see. This is how you connect with today's job seekers, who are online 24–7.

Consistent Messaging

Once you establish your employment brand, you must align all your communication so it's consistent with your brand. For example, suppose you are branding your organization as a company that treats its employees like family, yet you have no pictures of employees on your website. That would be the equivalent of an executive claiming to be a family man, yet not displaying photos of his family in his office or keeping them on his phone.

A picture is certainly worth a thousand words. Now, let's take this one step further. Stock photos on websites are great, but rarely do they actually look like the people you'll be hiring. The first thing a job seeker checks out when she's heard about an open position is the company's website. Let's face it, most of the photos on these sites are beautifully photoshopped. Job seekers usually take a few seconds before they say, "Hey, there is no one on this site who looks like me." And then they are off to check out the next job posting on someone else's website.

This is one time when perfection can hurt you. People with beautiful, shiny teeth do exist in Hollywood, thanks to prosthodontists, but the rest of the population usually has some imperfections. Consider asking your employees for permission to use photos taken of them in the workplace by a professional photographer. Most will be flattered that you asked. The outcome will be that much more powerful and will result in more people saying, "Hey, I can see myself working alongside these people, as we appear to have a lot in common."

Your branding has to carry through in everything you put out there, including recruitment materials, your website, social media outlets, the message delivered by your colleagues who are interviewing candidates, and, most importantly, the way you treat your people on a daily basis. Take this one step further and make sure all candidates, even those who aren't hired, leave your building singing the praises of your organization. It's not difficult to do if you treat every candidate as well as you treat your most valuable employees.

Communicating Your Brand

I've been in the business long enough to remember a time when a nice, fancy recruitment brochure was enough to get a candidate's attention. Nowadays, you need much more. Today's young candidates want to have a conversation with the people they will be working for. These conversations often take place on sites like Twitter. Others want to be able to experience what it would be like to work for an organization before they commit to the interview. This is where video can be extremely powerful. Having your employees share their stories (unscripted) is a great way for people to get a glimpse into what your organization is like. Some candidates may choose not to apply, but that's okay—you've saved yourself the time and expense of interviewing someone who would have most likely said, "No thanks."

A website is no longer a guarantee that people will know your company's name and story, as everyone has a website. Let's face it, some of you probably haven't updated your websites since the day they were launched, so you may be grateful to know that few are viewing your site right now.

It's easy to stand out in the crowd these days because most companies are taking the position that if a candidate really wants a job, they'll do whatever it takes to find out about an opportunity. You wouldn't believe the number of times I'm asked where else a company should be posting their opening when in fact they've never bothered to post the job on their own website. Will companies still take this posture when they wake up and realize it's no longer an employer's market?

Extreme Videos

A word of caution about using video: you can go overboard and turn people off. A gaming company reached out to me while I was researching this book and asked to be included. At first glance, it looked like the company had done a super job of standing out among the hundreds of other sites I have visited. The video on the home page describing the company culture appeared to be quite creative. About ten seconds into the video, I became mesmerized, but not for the right reasons. The script included a bunch of curse words that would have given the video at least an R rating if it were shown at a cinema. I left the site puzzled about who exactly the company was trying to attract. I knew for sure it wasn't anyone over the age of twenty-five. I guess they made their point and did a great job of screening people out who wouldn't be comfortable working there, but they also missed a great PR opportunity. The name of the company does not appear in this book, nor will I make specific mention of that business in future postings for *Fast Company*, *Forbes*, or any other publication I might write for.

Communicating your brand makes good business sense. Not only will you attract great job candidates, you will also attract new customers to your business as you continue to get the word out about your company.

Websites

The main problem I've seen with using websites to communicate your employment brand—and this is a problem particularly in small and medium-sized businesses—is that the career section of the site is usually an afterthought. Someone is tasked with creating a page that links to some boring job descriptions that would make almost anyone think twice about applying. I've even seen some company career pages that don't tell candidates how to apply for a job! Hopefully,

I'm not talking about your company's website. But just in case I am, you'd better check your site.

The person in charge of the page throws in a few stock photos for good measure, and the company considers the page good to go until the next time the site is redone. Many forget that you have to maintain those career pages. You must add new jobs and remove positions that are filled, unless you really are hiring a Santa Claus in April!

Always keep your end goal in mind. The object of your web presence, from a recruiting prospective, is to tell your story and explain the type of talent you're looking for. By putting it all out there, you will eliminate those candidates who aren't a good cultural fit and will attract those who are.

Great career pages often list the many benefits of working with the firm (many of these aren't financial), and they use photos to convey their message. For example, one company that allows employees to bring pets to work has photos of these four-legged "employees." If you are an animal lover, you don't need to read any further. You already know you've found a place that you and Fido can call home.

Here's what I recommend to my clients regarding creating a career section that stands out in a crowded field.

- ⟲ Assemble a team of employees who are representative of your brand and ask them to work together to design your career pages.

- ⟲ Bring in an outside employment-branding expert to guide the team through this process.

- ⟲ Provide examples of career pages that you feel work well, so the team isn't working in the dark.

- ⟲ Ask the team to come up with suggestions and ideas for your site. Encourage them to include video, photos of employees (with their permission, of course), and social media buttons that allow visitors to the site to easily share information and open positions with others.

C Provide a budget so the team can hire the resources (e.g., videographer, professional photographer, etc.) required to project the image you are trying to achieve.

C Assign an IT person in your firm who can serve as the technology specialist.

C Set a deadline. This shouldn't take years to complete.

Social Media

It's not enough these days to have a web presence. You must be where the job seekers are hanging out. As of this writing, LinkedIn is the place where the business sector networks. Of course, given the rapid changes common in the social media landscape, that could change tomorrow. Most of you probably have social media experts either employed in your organization or residing in your home. It's a good idea to check in with them frequently to stay abreast of the changes in this new media.

Facebook fan pages are a great way to connect with job seekers, especially young, passive job seekers, as Facebook tends to attract a younger crowd than LinkedIn. Facebook plug-ins like Work for Us allow you to create a customized job board on your Facebook page. Job seekers can submit résumés through the app or be redirected to a company's career website. Recruiters can also create custom Facebook ad campaigns to target specific segments of candidates based on attributes like location, education, and interests.

LinkUp is another app worth exploring. This application automatically feeds your jobs daily from your company's website to your Facebook page. When you add, remove, or edit a job on your website, the information is automatically updated, without any additional work.

The great thing about using social media to recruit is that it's fairly low risk. You don't have to invest a ton of money to get started, and you can always abandon your approach for one that gives you better results, should you find a method that better suits your organization.

College Campuses

On-campus recruiting is still popular among companies hiring a large number of entry-level professionals every year. It's always a good idea to bring employees from your company who are alums of the school you are visiting, as that will allow prospective employees to learn firsthand about the success of one of their own. Streaming your company's story on an iPad and showing your employees engaged both at work and in social situations is a great way to connect with young people, as most are visually oriented. Some companies go as far as to hire former interns to act as company ambassadors and encourage like-minded students to visit their company's booth at career fairs and apply for work with the company they represent.

Giveaways with company logos are still quite popular among college recruits. Check with the college career office to see what's in and what's not, so you don't wind up investing in a giveaway that gets tossed in the trash before students even leave the room.

The Community

Where better to look for good people than in your own community? You'll meet like-minded individuals through volunteering or by sitting on the board of a local nonprofit. Be sure to send out press releases to your local paper regarding newsworthy events in your business. This will help spread the word about your company and will continue to keep you top of mind with candidates who may be considering a move to your company.

Groups and Associations

You cannot simply join a business association and expect to reap the many benefits associated with membership. You must get involved. Take a look at the associations you belong to and make a decision to get involved, or replace that association with one where you have an interest in being involved. Take responsibility for programs that will put you in touch with prospective recruits for your organization. This can be rewarding both personally and professionally.

Sponsoring an on-campus college club is a terrific way to keep your company name in front of potential graduates and to help students in majors that are of interest to you. Contact the office of the president at schools where you may have an interest in developing relationships and ask what the next steps might be to support an on-campus club. Some clubs may welcome speakers, so be sure to offer to speak if you are looking to make a lasting impression on tomorrow's workforce.

Your Employee Pipeline

There is no better way to get your company's brand out there than through your employees, both current and past. Companies like Zappos and Kimpton Hotels encourage their employees to maintain Twitter accounts. Some encourage employees to blog daily about nonconfidential work-related matters. Both small and large organizations offer bonuses for employees who refer people who are hired. Most of the major CPA firms have alumni associations that encourage referrals of job candidates as well as new business. You've got a pool of talented people waiting to sing your praise. Continue to treat them well and encourage them to share their happiness with the world around them. A note of caution: if you need to let your social media manager go, remember to take him off your Twitter account before doing so!

Public Relations Agencies

It never hurts to have help, especially if you are gearing up for some major hiring. A good PR agency can help you spread the word near and far. Ask several trusted colleagues for the names of firms they have used. Keep in mind that it takes time for PR to work, so continue to spread the word on your own—you don't want to lose momentum.

Beauty Contests and Employment Brands

I always suspected that there was more to the "Best Place to Work" awards scene than met the eye and I was right. In fact, today there are so many of these lists that being named is no longer what it used to be. Yet employers still spend tons of cash in their attempts to be awarded this fading badge of honor.

Joanne Cleaver—who designed methodology to rank the Fortune 500 according to how well women fared in their executive ranks for *Working Woman* magazine, and who translated the methodology for women's associations in various industries—wrote a piece for *CBS Moneywatch* that revealed a number of secrets, including:

- Very few list-makers ask for statistical evidence that programs are actually used by significant numbers of employees or that the programs actually drive business results. Do you really want to be associated with a list that may be beautiful from the outside but empty on the inside?

C Nearly all list-makers take companies' self-reported answers at face value. Companies like Novartis, which lost a class-action discrimination suit for paying female sales reps less than their male counterparts and for demoting pregnant female employees, still managed to make it onto the "100 Best Companies for Working Mothers" list. As of 2012, they were still on the list! If you hire people who aren't smart enough to Google the companies on this list, then I guess you'll get what you deserve.

C There is a cost to appear on these free lists. These costs are described as "application fees" or administrative fees. For example, the U.K.'s *Sunday Times* "Best Companies to Work For" list requires an investment of $1,500 (for companies with fifty employees) to $4,700 (for companies with 5,000 employees) to cover the administrative costs. These numbers are based on today's exchange rate and become even greater as you add more employees. Some of the best companies in the world may choose not to pay to play. So will this list really result in the 100 best or just the 100 best that are willing to pay their way to the top?

C Most companies that hit the list feel compelled to pay their list-maker more money to advertise their placement on the list. Wouldn't this money be better spent on rewarding your employees for a job well done? A side benefit to doing so will be all those tweets going out telling everyone that your company really is a great place to work.

My advice is to skip the beauty contest scene and have people appreciate your company for who you truly are. In the long run, you'll be a lot happier and you won't be forced to do work on your organization that only goes skin deep.

Four Surefire Ways to Make Your Employment Brand Unattractive

There are a lot more than four ways to blow up the brand you've worked so hard to create. In the interest of time and your sanity, let's focus on four big ones.

1. Bad Candidate Experiences

Nothing says, "Stay the heck away from these people" faster than a bad candidate experience. I had the privilege of experiencing one of these for myself more than twenty-five years ago. I still talk about it today when I'm speaking to CEOs and association members about what not to do when you are building your employment brand.

I'm sharing my story so that you don't make a similar mistake. I was interviewing with American Express in Ft. Lauderdale for a position in one of its prestigious training programs. I spent an entire day being shifted from office to office because no one had time to interview me. I spent the next day going on a housing tour, although no one stopped long enough to even ask me if I was interested in the job. I left Florida shaking my head.

The company made me an offer and I turned it down. The next day I received a call from the VP of Human Resources, who was not in the office the day that I interviewed. He was stunned that I turned down the offer. He told me that no one turns down American Express. My reply, "You people didn't have time to interview me. How will you have time to train me?" He was silent for a moment and then said, "You know, you are right."

Naturally, I told my friends and many others not to bother to interview in what was, at the time, a very crazy place. Today, that message would have traveled halfway around the globe in less than twenty-four hours, as job seekers think nothing of sharing their interviewing experiences with anyone who is willing to give them an ear.

Treat candidates like you'd like to be treated. Begin and end interviews on time. Turn off your cell phone. Make the candidate feel welcome. At the end of the interview, tell candidates the next step. Then follow through as promised. Simple, right? Then, be the exception. Actually follow up.

2. Lies, Lies, Lies

Would you stick around if you knew the people above you were constantly lying? I'd like to think not. So many companies damage their reputations through lies. As CEO or other senior executive, you may not be lying to your people, but that doesn't necessarily mean those below you are following your lead. Here's a line that was taken out of Glassdoor, an online site that offers job seekers an inside look at companies: "Lies. Pay was a lie, job description was a lie, and training for a GM position was nonexistent."

Did you for a moment think this review might have been about your company? If so, you have work that needs to be done.

3. Layoffs

I've worked with enough companies to know that many choose to "lay off" employees rather than confront poor performers and fire them. These companies have no idea the damage the term *layoff* can do when they eventually decide to rehire for a position or they are able to turn things around and grow again. Fire bad performers now, and you may not have to consider a company-wide layoff.

When it comes to promises, learn a lesson from Big Blue (IBM), which for years touted the fact that it had a no-layoff policy. That was until 1993, when the company announced it was ending the policy. Never promise people what you cannot deliver. If someone asks if cuts are in store and you are fairly certain they may be, tell the person that everything is being looked at right now. Remember, no lies.

The Difficult Task of Letting People Go

Davidd Gammel, executive director of the Entomological Society of America, never takes firing someone lightly. "Letting someone go is a major disruption in someone's life," states Gammel. He goes on to say, "Just because it's hard, doesn't mean you shouldn't do it. We cannot afford to have any dead wood on the staff. Poor attitudes really pull everyone down and suck up a lot of time that we don't have." Gammel advises business leaders to take action when people aren't contributing, especially if the struggling employee cannot be remediated or developed any further. Then they have to go.

"It's your duty to the organization and the rest of the staff to do this, and it is ultimately in the best interest of the person to do so as well," notes Gammel.

---

4. Treating Third-Party Recruiters Poorly

Most companies treat third-party recruiters, often referred to as headhunters, as vendors instead of partners. How do I know this? People in your company are on association boards, proudly pounding their chests because they were able to squeeze another 1 percent off the fee these recruiters earn (and I do mean *earn*.)

You wouldn't ask your most critical supplier to shave a percentage point off his fees, especially if you knew it would affect the quality of the product you would be receiving. The same holds true for recruiters. Companies that pay full freight are sent the cream of the crop. Those paying the "sale price" will receive yesterday's goods. And if that weren't bad enough, some recruiters will tarnish your brand by telling candidates that your company isn't the most generous.

Treat your third-party recruiters well, and they will do the same for you and your brand.

Rule of Attraction

Brands—especially employment brands—are about perception. People are attracted by a compelling promise. What does your employment brand say about your organization? An employment brand is as important as your product branding and should not be treated as an afterthought. Invest the time and resources necessary to create an employment brand that connects emotionally with those whom you are trying to pull in.

CHAPTER

The Leader As a Talent Magnet

Employees don't work for companies. They work for people. If this is all you take away from this book, you will have learned something of incalculable value. Too many business owners, CEOs, and senior executives operate their organizations without any regard for the people side of the business. Things are fine as long as the numbers look fine. But what if cultivating your staff made the numbers look significantly better over a longer period of time? Would you then pay attention to your people?

I've always been puzzled as to why it appears that few CEOs are concerned about employee turnover, so I asked Mark Triest, president of Ex Libris North America, to shed some light on this subject. "CEOs and executives do care, and they know deep down inside that losing people who have unique skills and a great deal of knowledge costs the company a great deal of money. The people side is the hardest side to deal with, so some executives choose not to deal with it." Triest goes on to say that it's easy to fix an operations problem. You identify what needs to be done, and you have someone do it. This certainly isn't the case when you have to figure out how to resolve a personnel issue.

But this is what magnetic leaders do. They understand that people stay and are committed to their employers because of their immediate boss and the leadership of the company. They make it so darn hard to leave because their people know they'll never be treated this well again.

The Paranormal Powers of Magnetic Leaders

Chris Patterson, CEO and owner of Interchanges—a company based in Jacksonville, Florida, that helps clients achieve revenue growth through groundbreaking marketing systems—is a magnetic leader. I've had a number of conversations with Patterson over the years as he's struggled with the same issues many of you have in your businesses. But one thing Patterson doesn't struggle with is magnetism. "I took note all along when I was an employee regarding what I liked and didn't like as an employee. And that's how I built my company," claims Patterson.

He operates his company from his heart and is one of the most ethical people I know. He believes it's important for the leader of the organization to get to really know his people as individuals. Patterson makes it a point to invite staff members and their families to his home and to thank the spouses who are often left at home to tend to family members while their partner is working late. He does so by purchasing gifts and sending them along with a personalized note thanking the spouses or significant others for their support. He does this because he wants to, not because he has to.

Patterson and I discussed how he is able to make these types of gestures because his company is small and agile. We also noted that a larger company would have a much bigger budget to send elaborate gifts, should it choose to do so. A larger company would also likely have more staff on hand so that people wouldn't have to work too many late nights or weekends. It's really about making a choice. As a leader, are you going to do whatever is in your power to improve the lives of your team members or are you going to try to squeeze every nickel from your people's paycheck? Your response to this question will have a direct impact on your legacy, which at the end of the day is all you have.

It should come as no surprise that voluntary turnover at Interchanges is extremely low. We'll talk more about why this is so in the chapters related to employee retention.

Magnetic Leader Paul Kraemer

Paul Kraemer—regional employer group segment CEO for the East Region for Kentucky-based Humana, one of the nation's leading health and wellness companies—is another magnetic leader who stands out as both memorable and irresistible. I've worked with Kraemer over the years as he's moved from one company to another. I've personally observed his interactions with his employees and have always walked away impressed.

I'm never surprised to hear that those employees Kraemer has left behind soon find their way back to him. Think about it. How many bosses have left such a positive impression on you that you would follow them to their next venture? If you are like most people, the answer would be "not many."

"I do everything I can to make my people successful in their roles at Humana. My ultimate goal is for them to be happy in their jobs at Humana, so their well-being both inside and outside work is enhanced by the work they do in our company." Kraemer goes on to say, "My approach is the same at work as it is outside work. I treat everyone the same, whether it's the CEO of Humana or the janitor in our office building. They see me as real. People see me as real. People aren't afraid to share their ideas with me, nor are they afraid to fail. It's a comfortable environment and I think that's what people like about working with me. The key word here is 'with' me."

Traits Associated with Magnetic Leaders

I've been fortunate to have encountered some incredibly magnetic leaders and have personally observed what makes them different from their peers. Here are some of my observations.

Magnetic leaders are more concerned with the well-being of others than with their own wealth. CEO Chris Patterson demonstrates this every day. He is always asking himself what he can do to better support those who work for him. In return, his people are committed to him and to his company. I remember a conversation in which Patterson was expressing concern about what his employees would think if he arrived at work in a Bentley. He struggled for a while, trying to decide whether to make such an extravagant purchase. In the end, Patterson's colleagues reminded him that he deserved to treat himself well, as he was the person taking risks every day, and obviously these risks were paying off handsomely.

Patterson decided to purchase the car. He bravely drove his Bentley to work and received a reaction that he never anticipated. His employees were thrilled to see him drive up in such a nice vehicle. I'm sure many were lining up for rides. They surrounded him and congratulated him on purchasing his dream car.

Now, compare this reaction to the one most CEOs get when they show up in the company parking lot with a new Mercedes or BMW: employees making snide comments either behind their backs or to their faces. Soon thereafter, people start coming in asking for raises. The list goes on. Rarely do you hear of a group of employees rallying around the boss and saying, "Hey, you've always taken care of us. We are thrilled you are finally taking care of yourself." Try putting your employees' needs before your own. Their reaction will be remarkable.

Magnetic leaders also treat people as individuals, not as if they were one of the masses. I tell my clients that equal isn't always fair. Here's what I mean by that. Suppose you have a dedicated employee who is always there when you need her. One day, this person makes a request of you that doesn't fit company policy: she asks you if she can work from home one day a week so that she can take her ill mother to her weekly doctor's appointment. A magnetic leader would look at the situation and wouldn't think twice. He would say, "Of course," because he understands that if you give your all to your best performers, they in turn will give the same to you.

Magnetic leaders have a real connection with their people that remains even after the workday is officially over. But all too often leaders begin thinking about the precedent granting such a request might set. They immediately think that the floodgates will open. (And what if they do?) So instead, many decline the request, using the company line, "Our company policy doesn't allow this." That one line changes the dynamics of your relationship with the employee forever.

Magnetic leaders examine individual situations with an eye toward doing whatever they can to grant employees' wishes. They know it's the right thing to do from a human perspective. (Don't forget, employees are human.) The leaders then figure out a way to make things right with other employees, if they feel they must do so. This may include reviewing company policies to make sure they still make sense and are meeting the needs of the changing workforce, as well as the company. They also know that employees work for people, not companies. These employees will certainly think twice before accepting an invitation to interview elsewhere because they know how good they have it at their current place of employment.

Magnetic leaders have high self-esteem. They are confident leaders. They make the tough decisions that need to be made, with little thought about how others will view their decisions. For example, magnetic leaders will promote an individual because that person is deserving of a promotion, even if it's not the most popular thing to do. They'll do whatever is necessary to support this person and will help her shine, even if it means the spotlight is no longer on them.

Magnetic Leader Peter Rinnig

Peter Rinnig, owner of QRST's, a custom and digital printing business based in Somerville, Massachusetts, goes way beyond the norm when it comes to treating employees as individuals. Here's an example of how he caters to the needs of one of his employees: "I have an employee by the name of Paul who goes on tour every summer with his band. He goes for six or seven weeks. He doesn't get paid while he is gone, but he knows he has his job when he gets back. He knows that no one else will do that for him."

As an added bonus, Rinnig gives Paul (and any other employee) the right to use company equipment, as long as he does so on his own time. With permission, employees can print their own items on his press, provided they don't compete with him. As a result of this arrangement, Paul prints band T-shirts that are sold when the band is on tour. And, more importantly to Paul, he's able to pursue his dreams without worrying that he'll be replaced when he returns, which is usually right before the fall rush. This situation works well for Rinnig, as he knows he can count on Paul giving his all when he's back at QRST's manning his post, and he's fairly confident that Paul will stick around for a while, as most employers would never even consider such an arrangement.

The Power of Magnetic Leadership

There are many benefits associated with magnetic leadership. Some you may know about, while others aren't that obvious. They include the following advantages.

Ease of Recruitment

When it comes to attracting talent, active, engaged, and innovative leaders provide a key competitive advantage. The magnetism they possess creates a powerful draw for potential workers and, in many cases, customers. This magnetism is almost impossible to break.

"Hiring people is easier because people do want to work for a magnetic leader," states Humana executive Paul Kraemer. "Your pool of candidates is broader. People will tell their peers, and they will refer them to you when you have a job opening. These candidates are usually a good fit because they are being recommended to you by people who know you." Kraemer goes on to point out that once these people are on board, the fact that they were brought in by someone they know enhances loyalty. In his experience, those who are referred often perform better and are happier at work. "This makes the entire work environment more fun and successful," says Kraemer.

Companies with reputations for strong leadership have a much easier time getting people to come on board than those with tarnished reputations or no reputation to speak of. Nowhere is this more evident than at General Electric (GE). The mere mention of Jack Welch, who in 1999 was named the "Manager of the Century" by *Fortune* magazine, caused people to flock to GE. Welch's name is still closely aligned with the GE brand, which continues to be perceived in the marketplace as a great place to work, even years after Welch's 2001 retirement from the company. His legacy at GE lives on.

Ed Moore, CEO of Harrington Hospital, a regional hospital based in Southbridge, Massachusetts, firmly believes that his reputation as a leader has made it easier for him to recruit strong talent for his organization, which in turn keeps his stress levels down. "It's easier to recruit because we look like a team who has their act together. We have a lot of success stories that have played out favorably." Moore goes on to say, "People know we are not just full of air. We are real. Our dreams have come true because we work together to make this so." He asks candidates if they want to be part of an organization that has dreams and gets things done. For most people, the answer is yes. The others need not apply.

Reduced Hiring Costs

Think of the money your organization spends every time you *attempt* to fill a position. Tangible costs include the cost of advertising, Internet posting, employment agencies, search firms, employee referral awards, hosting out-of-town candidates, assessment testing, background checks, drug screening (usually done on more than one candidate), and so on. You can then add intangible costs, such as opportunity costs, stress, and other matters going south as you focus on filling this hole in your organization. And there is no guarantee that your effort will yield the results you seek.

Now, imagine for a moment how much money you could keep in the company coffers if you were able to significantly reduce the time and cost associated with hiring the right people. This number is substantial, no matter how big or small your business is.

Executives who make it a point to personally reach out to candidates whom they've had their eye on are often able to capture the talent they need without handing over 30 percent of the candidate's first-year salary to a search firm. Multiply this number a few times over, and you can see immediately the benefit when leaders are able to easily pull talent into their field of attraction without using outside resources.

High Levels of Employee Commitment

Employees who work for magnetic leaders have a strong personal connection to these leaders and are willing to go above and beyond the call of duty without ever being asked. They do their best work because they want to, not because they are in fear of losing their jobs.

Contrary to popular belief, you cannot make someone commit to you, nor can you make him stay committed. Commitment comes from trust. When trust levels are high, there is no telling what people will do when someone asks.

Staff Productivity That Is Out of This World

Along with great leadership comes high levels of productivity. When you work for a great leader, you don't waste countless hours watching the clock. Instead, you ponder ways that you can improve the product or service you are working on. The engagement (and productivity) of your own people escalates as you model the behaviors of your own boss.

Humana's Paul Kraemer has had many star performers work for him at a number of organizations. Some might consider this a coincidence. And perhaps it would be if it happened twice, but Kraemer has overseen top-rate talent again and again, which means it's a pattern. Strong performers seek enlightened leadership and an environment where they feel cared for. Studies support this notion. Kraemer and Humana continue to prove it day in and day out.

Magnetic Leaders Are True to Their Word

Ed Moore, CEO of Harrington Hospital, doesn't need to spend much time convincing people they should take a job at his hospital or remain in the hospital's employ. That's because Moore demonstrates why it's in the other person's best interest to work alongside Moore day in and day out through his interactions all around the hospital system. He says, "I've recruited many people who used to work for me, and they come along willingly because they trust me. They remember that I've always done what I told them I would do." Moore goes on to say, "They know I'm honest, trusting, and legitimate. I'm not a micromanager."

Moore shared stories of many different employees he had the good fortune of working with more than one time. One story, in particular, demonstrates how far some people will go to work for a great leader. Moore reached out to a former employee who had young children at home and asked her to join his team at Harrington Hospital. She agreed, in spite of a ninety-minute commute each way. She did the commute for a number of years because Moore told her that he had a great opportunity for her and she believed him. And you know what? It was true. She recently moved to be closer to the hospital.

A common thread among magnetic leaders is honesty and transparency. Moore asked me why I thought this was so difficult for leaders to do. I have to admit, I couldn't answer his question. Nor could he, when I turned the question back to him.

Magnetic Leaders Truly Enjoy What They Do

I've worked for some leaders who you just knew were doing their jobs purely for the money. The only fun they ever had at work was making other people squirm. Ed Moore points out that some industries, like health care, can be miserable to work in. He understands that it can be difficult for people to come to work every day ready to do their best when the environment is dismal. The ever-changing world of health-care delivery, with all of its cuts, has contributed to increased stress in many hospital settings. His motto is, "Let's have fun doing this." He makes himself directly accessible and creates the type of environment where people feel good about their work. He does this by providing them with what they most value: an opportunity to be in control of their work and to grow in their careers. This flows from the top of the organization to the bottom.

I remember the first time I walked into Harrington Hospital to meet with Moore. I dashed into the ladies' room just before our meeting and heard what sounded like angels singing. At first I thought perhaps I had mistakenly walked into the hospital chapel. But I knew I was in the right place when I encountered a woman cleaning the restroom. It was her voice I had heard. She was smiling and singing away as she did what most would find to be quite a monotonous job. How many people in your business are truly happy and singing your praises? If you can't think of one, then we really need to talk.

During our interview, Moore explained that he knows that the people he hires have lots of other options. "They could work anywhere and make a lot more money easily," said Moore. He also knows that those who work under his direction do so because of the personal connection they feel to him and, even more importantly, because most days they are having fun at work. I'll let you in on a secret. His people aren't the only ones having fun. Moore is having the time of his life as well.

How You Can Create a Force of Magnetic Leaders

What if you could create a magnetic force field around your most talented people that others couldn't penetrate? You can, and you don't need to have a PhD in science to do so.

You just need common sense. The results of several recent Gallup studies on employee turnover indicated that managers can influence 75 percent of the reasons for voluntary turnover. Simply put, this means that you have to have the right team of managers in place to keep people engaged, which in turn will prevent others from breaking through and snagging your best people. Here is how you make this happen.

Throw poor managers back into orbit. Begin by doing an honest evaluation of your current management team. For many of you, this will require removing managers who should never have been hired in the first place. Others may have peaked, and may have lost interest either this decade or last. Send these people on the next flight out of your organization. Next, replace these managers with "A" players. With just one magnetic leader, you will be able to more easily attract other leaders with equal levels of magnetism. Why? Because their pull is so strong.

I've been fortunate to work for someone I consider a magnetic leader. I was always impressed by the caliber of the managers he was able to pull into his company, especially because his business was in an industry that wasn't considered all that appealing. I mean, really, how many people do you know who dream about working in the overnight delivery business? I can count the number on one hand. Here is what I noticed that this leader and others like him did particularly well.

They all hired right the first time around—they were patient. To an outsider, the hiring process at the company I worked for may have seemed a bit much, but to this leader, it was exactly right. You see, he was working with a tight-knit team, and he knew that every person he added would change the dynamics. He had to be 100 percent sure that this change would be one that would propel his organization in the direction he wanted it to go. And it did, just about every time.

This CEO believed that two heads were better than one. Candidates who made it through the initial phone screening were invited in for an interview, which, depending on the level of hire, may have been conducted by several members of the team. A select few were then invited to meet with other team members as well. This second round of interviews gave the candidates a chance to get to know those people they would be working with. And it also sometimes caused eager hiring managers to rethink their decisions based on input that others gave them.

Now, you might be thinking, "I don't have time for this in my organization." But this CEO made sure his people made the time for such an important decision, which is what exceptional CEOs do. In an interview for a piece that I wrote for Monster's small business community, I spoke with Dan Yates, CEO and cofounder of Opower, a U.S.-based provider of customer engagement platforms for the utility industry, to learn more about how he's been able to successfully staff a high-growth company. Yates believes the secret formula to small business success is hiring the right people. "We've hired really talented people and have given them the responsibility and the authority, as well as great coworkers," states Yates. The company looks for "A" players and has the patience and discipline to wait for the right person, rather than settling. "A people hire A people. B people hire C people," notes Yates.

Assess leaders frequently. It's important to evaluate your leaders on a regular basis. This will allow you to offer them additional support to boost their performance or to provide them with feedback regarding their areas of strength as well as those areas that need further development. It's also important to do this so you can quickly remove people who are no longer up to the challenge.

However, I see many organizations in which leaders, once ordained, are allowed to rule until someone finally knocks them off their throne. That's because their boss is operating under the old school of management that says, "If I don't hear any complaints, everything is fine." That is, until the staff goes wild and plans a coup. Only, you don't hear about it until it's too late.

Support the development of leaders. There are no short-cuts when it comes to leadership development. Handing mangers a book to read (even if it's authored by me) isn't going to get them where they need to be at the speed you need them to get there. Nor is sending them to a one-day workshop at the local Holiday Inn. To be effective, leaders need ongoing support. For years, many CEOs and other senior executives have experienced firsthand the benefits of working with a coach. Today, many forward-thinking organizations (both for-profit and nonprofit) are seeing the light and providing this type of support to their people. Their investment in coaching is reaping dividends year in and year out.

In my book *Suddenly in Charge* (Nicholas Brealey, 2011), Mary Duseau, former vice president of global sales and marketing at Bio-discovery PerkinElmer Human Health, notes the commitment that world leader PerkinElmer makes in the development of its people, especially those who are considered star performers:

> At PerkinElmer Human Health, we provide coaches to many of our incredibly valuable employees. This is an investment we are making in them. Each employee has a 5 percent development goal to work toward, whether with a coach or not, in order to take the next step. That 5 percent is usually very personal; for example, smoothing an edge, finding ways to be more confident, or improving executive articulation and presentation. I can—and do—help with these things, but I've found that it's more digestible coming from a third party. I

can see a measurable improvement month by month when someone is working with a coach. But I recognize that this is a work in progress, and that we must continually work together to keep things moving in the right direction.

My best clients always go the extra mile and provide their valuable employees with coaching. In fact, a new client of mine is about to inform another lucky leader that she has been selected to receive this valuable gift. This investment will pay off in a number of ways, including cementing the employee's relationship with her manager as well as with the organization. You should be doing the same to strengthen your team's performance and to create a force field that will prevent talent from being pulled right out from under you.

Rule of Attraction

Put pencil to paper and list all of the magnetic leaders who reside in your organization. If this exercise causes you to pull out an additional piece of paper, then you are well on your way to creating an army of magnetic leaders. If you can't think of any or you only have a handful, then seek a trusted adviser who will be brutally honest and tell you what you need to know, rather than what you may want to hear.

CHAPTER

Creating a Magnetic Interviewing Process

A ttraction is a two-way street, yet many organizations fail to recognize that top candidates (all candidates, for that matter) are deciding whether the organization is deserving of them. This conversation is taking place inside the heads of candidates, regardless of the state of the economy.

I graduated from college at a time when jobs were extremely difficult to find. Yet, even at a young age, I knew that if I didn't pay attention to the signals that companies were throwing off throughout the interviewing process, I would be back on the street before too long. I wasn't willing to jump from a job that was fairly mindless to one where I would have to use a machete to cut through bureaucracy, a bureaucracy that was well represented in the interviewing process.

It's been a considerable number of years since my experience interviewing for jobs after college graduation, though from what I've seen, little has changed. Here is my list of the eleven most common mistakes that turn candidates off and what you can do to avoid being known as that company no one wants to interview with. Or, worse yet, the company no one wants to work for.

1. Creating a Wall Around Your Company

Is there a barrier around your company that requires heavy artillery to penetrate? I've heard CEOs and business owners proudly flaunt the fact that it's extremely difficult to get an interview with their company. Yet, these same people are the first to complain that there is a shortage of skilled workers or that they are having a difficult time filling a particular position. Here's a news flash. If a top-flight candidate happens to come across your company and can't easily locate the name of the hiring manager or any mention of where to send her résumé, she'll be in the arms of the next suitor before you even realize that you've lost your chance.

Remove the barriers that are preventing candidates from pursuing you. At a minimum, make sure your company website includes easy-to-find instructions for how candidates can apply for work with your firm. You'd be amazed how many company websites don't have this information on their sites, even though they are advertising elsewhere that they are hiring. Before you move on to the next paragraph, take a few minutes and visit your own company's website and apply for a position. If it takes more than ninety seconds to find the place to apply for a job, you've got a problem that needs to be fixed immediately.

2. Removing the Human Touch from the Hiring Process

Recruiting is a business strategy that, if handled properly, can yield dramatic results. But in most organizations, recruitment is treated like a necessary evil and is usually handed off to the HR department, where either nonhumans (applicant tracking systems) or low-level employees are tasked with screening candidates. The problem with most hiring processes is that they are meant to screen candidates out, rather than screen candidates in.

"Screening candidates" is usually code for sifting through résumés and giving the hiring manager the ones that have the keywords the manager wants to see. The problem with these systems is that anyone can game them. All candidates have to do is insert keywords, which can be extracted directly from the job posting, into their résumés, and they usually slide right through the system.

Sifting through hundreds of résumés yourself can be a daunting task. But if you take the time to do so, you will be amazed at some of the gems that may have been discarded had you delegated this task, especially if you are looking to make a key hire. Take this one step further by connecting personally with candidates who appear to be exactly what you are looking for, and you are on your way to beginning a real conversation with a candidate who will appreciate the fact that you took the time to respond personally. That is something that happens very rarely these days.

3. Shielding Those Responsible for Hiring

It's a mistake to shield managers from the people they are trying to hire. Would you allow your sales team to have someone else be the face of your organization with prospects and clients? Probably not. Yet some companies shield the people who are responsible for managing a team from the hiring process. Believe it or not, there are still some companies where HR and a designee in the department do all the hiring. Those candidates who make it through the process are then assigned to a manager. The manager has absolutely no say in who is selected, yet the manager is responsible for the performance of this person as well as the team. Crazy, eh?

How committed would you be to the success of an employee you had no relationship with? How quickly would you blame the process or the guy who made the offer for mistakes this person made, when in fact they were caused by something you did? At the end of the day, people have to be accountable for their actions. You cannot hold people accountable for something they weren't involved with.

4. Preventing Candidates from Meeting Their Managers

This goes back to point number three, but now we're looking at it from the candidate's point of view. Arranged marriages are still part of some cultures, and of course a number of these marriages do work out. But that doesn't mean that you have a whole bunch of people all over the world itching to spend the rest of their lives together because someone else thought it was a good idea. The same holds true when matching up candidates and their managers. I'm sure a few of these situations work out, but I'm guessing that a great many more of these relationships would last longer if the employee had actually met the person he'd be working for before saying, "I do."

There is a lot to be said for chemistry. A manager who gives very specific directions may be a good fit for someone who isn't particularly organized. However, the relationship would not work if an employee who prided herself on her ability to take the ball and run with it was assigned to this type of detail-oriented leader. Of course, an employee wouldn't know what kind of manager she was truly getting if she never met the person before being hired. At a minimum, bring both parties together for a face-to-face meeting, or, if that's not possible, arrange for a Skype call so a candidate has an opportunity to interact with the person she will be working with for, hopefully, a very long period of time.

5. Not Training Managers to Select Talent

Many of you reading this book have probably earned MBAs or at least an undergraduate degree in business. Did any of your management classes include hands-on sessions (or any session, for that matter) on how to select talent? I don't even recall that type of training being offered in companies with in-house management training programs.

In my experience, the majority of people responsible for hiring really don't have a clue as to what they are doing. Some get lucky and make some good hires, while the rest wind up in documentation hell, where they remain until such time as they've finally written up an employee enough times to get rid of him. Surely there is a better way. Every person (and that includes you) who is responsible for hiring should be properly trained in how to assess talent. It's too important a job to leave up to luck.

6. Posting Boring Job Descriptions

Some companies post job descriptions that make the position sound as exciting as being a weatherman in San Diego, where the forecast is the same every day. Many of you may not have even seen the job description written for your position, or you probably would have declined the offer to interview. My mentor, Alan Weiss, president of Summit Consulting Group, recommends replacing job descriptions with "results descriptions." These descriptions focus on results rather than activities and tasks. By describing what the person in this role is expected to accomplish (results), you will connect in a way that is different from 99 percent of the rest of the world, which is still using generic descriptions to attempt to connect with unique individuals. Go ahead, give it a go and see what happens.

7. Being Guilty of the "I'll Call You" Syndrome

If only this were true. It's been more than twenty years and I'm still waiting for some companies to get back to me! Empty promises and broken hearts lead to tainted brands. I stopped buying the products of a number of companies that played this game with me. Why? Because I no longer trusted their brands. If you're not going to call someone, then don't tell candidates you will. We are all grown-ups here. Be truthful and simply say that you'll be pursing other candidates. Then shake hands and thank them for their time.

8. Failing to Remove Expired Job Postings

Imagine spending your valuable time applying for a position, only to discover that the job was filled months ago. This happens every day to candidates because companies can't be bothered to take postings down or, quite frankly, because the person responsible for doing so doesn't know how to do it. I've had clients who were guilty of this. When I probed further, I was told about the hoops one had to go through to get a posting taken down. There are work-arounds for everything. Figure it out and make it happen. Having out-of-date job postings on your website is like keeping bread on grocery store shelves past the expiration date. You are sending the message that you simply don't care. If you believe, as I do, that company image is important, assign someone you trust to get the job done correctly. Do it now.

9. Not Vetting Third-Party Recruiters

When you work with third-party recruiters, you must make sure their values are aligned with those of your company. When you place your job opening with a recruiter, that person and his firm become the face of your company. As in any industry, there are good people, and then there are those who give everyone a bad name. When selecting a third-party recruiter to represent your firm, choose wisely. Whenever possible, ask for referrals, and if you don't receive any, be sure you at least ask the agency to provide you with references. Then be sure to check them.

10. Playing Hard to Get

Some companies make the mistake of playing hard to get. They take far too long to make a decision or to extend an offer, forgetting that the candidate is evaluating them as well. If you want someone bad enough, let her know. Being quick to decide doesn't mean you aren't thorough. It just means you know what you want and how to get it.

11. Springing Last-Minute Surprises on Candidates

Job hunters don't like surprises, especially when they pop up at the last minute. I've seen companies play the bait-and-switch game, as if these slimy tactics were actually going to work. Here is an example: "We know you said your salary range was $50,000 to $60,000. We are delighted to offer you $30,000." Or, one of my favorites: "You're perfect for the job, which is now in Siberia." Surprises like these do no one any good, as it's highly unlikely a candidate looking for $50,000 is going to jump for joy and relocate her family to Siberia. Instead, she'll be sure to tell others who were thinking about applying for a job with your business the cold, hard facts about your company. Hopefully, she'll choose to do this privately rather than through her social network.

How to Design a Magnetic Hiring Process That Yields Results

The hiring process you put in place several years ago might have been fine then, but is it still working for you? Maybe when the process was created, you had only one office and now you have ten. Or perhaps your process predates the invention of the Internet. In any case, examining what you are currently doing with an eye toward improvement is a good thing to do every now and again.

A good place to begin is with those who have declined your offers. Most of these people will be honest and will tell you what you need to hear, rather than what you want to hear. You can then work backward to make course corrections.

Based on my years of experience and the feedback I have received from hundreds of applicants, you will most likely need to work on the following:

The process itself. Consider Occam's razor: the most direct path is best. Eliminate excess layers of approval that are bogging your company down. Instead, simplify the process, keeping in mind that the fewer obstacles (and the fewer people sticking their hands in the pot), the better. You'll be light on your feet and will be able to quickly capture the talent you need.

Job requisitions. Is this step really necessary? Perhaps it is for big companies, but I can't think of a darn good reason you need an official job requisition if you are running a small business and can count the people you employ on your fingers. In fact, large companies may also be able to rid themselves of this step if their hiring system is automated. Instead, you can simply check off the box that indicates the position has been approved and move it swiftly along to the person responsible for doing the hiring.

Job descriptions. We touched upon this earlier in this chapter and discussed why you may want to replace these with "results descriptions." Here's another reason this idea is worth further consideration: job descriptions are the basis on which job postings are written, and they're usually quite dull, task oriented, and full of legal jargon that no one reads. Not even your dog would apply to 99 percent of the postings that are used by companies these days, unless the employer is willing to throw a bone to those who apply. Whatever you decide to do, keep it simple, as most descriptions will eventually change depending on who takes the position. Also, keep these descriptions lively in case a prospective employee actually reads one before deciding whether to take the job.

Job postings. Think about what will make a job candidate say, "I could see myself in this job." To do so, you must be creative and appeal to the emotional side of candidates, which is what causes them to take action. Here are excerpts from job descriptions for the position of brewing manager in two different companies.

Company A	Company B
Brewing manager leads and motivates the overall operational team for the safe and effective operation, quality, cost, and maintenance of all brewing activities. Ensures high-quality products are produced cost effectively through maximizing operational efficiency.	Seeking an off-centered leader to orchestrate the symphony that is XYZ Brewing. The successful candidate must be a triple threat: bringing outstanding people leadership, technical excellence, and off-centeredness in the form of amazing fit with our culture. In loose terms, you will be leading/coaching/guiding/developing the awesome folks who make the stuff we all love.

If you could only apply to one of these jobs, which would it be? And if you could apply to both, would you even bother to do so?

The people involved in the hiring process. Sometimes companies have a problem deciding who needs to be involved in the hiring process, so they invite everyone. This can be confusing and intimidating to some job seekers, and it's confusing and unproductive for those pulled into the process who shouldn't have been there in the first place. Here is my advice: invite only those people who will truly have a say in who gets hired and who doesn't. If your culture is similar to that of SPARC, where everyone has a say, then it makes sense to involve the entire team. And, of course, be sure to include the person who will actually be supervising the new hire.

Phone screening. Phone screening should be part of every company's hiring process. I'm always amazed when a company decides to fire an employee soon after he is hired because he doesn't possess strong telephone skills. The company would know this had a hiring manager set aside the time to interview the person by phone. The manager could also stop sitting through countless interviews with people who should have never been invited in for an interview because they do not have the skills or traits the company is seeking. Some people tell me they don't have time to screen candidates by phone. I tell those people they'd have a heck of a lot more time to work on other matters if they invested the fifteen to thirty minutes on a phone call instead.

Hiring managers' skills. You wouldn't hand the keys to a forklift driver without making sure he had the skills to handle such heavy equipment, would you? Yet every day, thousands of managers are sent to the front lines and asked to conduct interviews without the skills required to make good hiring decisions; without developed hiring skills, there is every likelihood they will do damage to the company. Many executives tell me that, when it comes to hiring, they'll know it when they see it. These same executives are calling me weeks, months, and sometimes years later to help them coach or transition out of the organization a person they've hired. The ability to assess people for cultural fit and for skills isn't something we are born with. However, it certainly is something that people can learn. That is, if the organization is willing to invest time and money in teaching them how to do so. We'll talk about this more in the next chapter.

Alignment of values. Most of the memorable interviews I've had are the ones I'd rather forget. At these interviews, I was treated like I really didn't matter. So I treated these companies the same way by declining their offers. Begin by treating people the way you'd like to be treated. It sounds so simple, yet few companies actually do this, unless, of course, you like being prodded and made to feel that if you move along with the herd, one day you'll be noticed. Create a process in which all candidates are treated with respect, one that is personable and memorable for the right reasons.

Parting gifts. Over the years, I've interviewed with dozens of companies. One stands head and shoulders above the rest. The company was called the Coffee Connection, and it was quickly absorbed by Starbucks. At the end of the interview, the executive who interviewed me asked me to wait a moment while he went to grab something. He returned with a bag full of coffee beans. I can still close my eyes and remember the smell and the impression he made by offering me a gift. I didn't get the job, but I sure did enjoy the coffee that I brewed at home. Years later, I reconnected with this COO, and this time we did work together. What type of parting gift can you provide to all candidates as a way of thanking them for their time and showing them you are indeed worth further consideration?

The courtesy of a reply. Make sure to close the loop with candidates you've interviewed. Imagine what it must feel like to invest half a day of your time or, in many cases, even more, and never be told you didn't get the job. Of course, after a week, a month, or a few years' time, you've probably figured out that the job went to someone else. But wouldn't it have been nice to be told instead of hanging on for weeks thinking that perhaps the hiring manager lost your number while on safari in Africa? Here's the thing. A simple e-mail, voice-mail message, or even a form letter is better than no word at all. It may be uncomfortable for you to deliver this news, but this isn't about you. It's about the candidate getting closure. Do the right thing. Always close the loop.

Rule of Attraction

Is your interview process pulling good people in or repelling them? Don't know? Pick up the phone and personally call candidates who have recently turned down your offer and ask them why they decided not to come work for your company. When doing so, just listen and take note of what you can do to improve your process.

CHAPTER

Selecting for Success

I've spoken with hundreds of CEOs and business owners over the years, and all say that hiring the right people is critical for business success. Yet most admit that they've never been formally trained on how to select for success. Instead, they've relied on their gut, and most admit they have been wrong more often than they'd like to recall.

If you believe, like I do, that hiring the right people the first time can significantly increase productivity, profitability, and business growth, then read on. If you'd rather continue trusting your gut, then reread the chapters on attracting top talent to your organization. You'll need this information to replace those who aren't working out the way you'd hoped.

Does the following sound familiar?

"How did I not see that coming? I spent more than three hours with this guy, and I thought for sure he was the one. My problem employee sailed through the interviewing process and left a lasting impression on all of us."

This scenario plays out in workplaces all over the world. Few managers enjoy interviewing. Therefore, they enter the process with one goal in mind: to hire someone as quickly as possible so they can put this chore behind them. Sure, there might be a few warning lights going off about the candidate, but heck, no one is perfect!

It happens to the best of us, no matter how experienced we are at interviewing: we hire people we never should have hired. Some candidates are professional interviewers. They seem to have the right answer for every question. This may sound particularly familiar if you are hiring salespeople, who are usually quite good at selling themselves. Then there are those we hired because we are not as skilled at assessing candidates as we need to be.

You can significantly minimize the likelihood that someone will slip through the cracks if you follow this magnetic interviewing process, which I call Selecting for Success.

Why Hire for Fit?

Exceptional organizations select and retain exceptional people. It makes no difference whether you are an accounting firm, football team, or retail operation—people are what differentiate your business from the competition. People are what make a particular organization outstanding!

But the people who make up a great accounting firm may not be the best players for a football team. That's because the activities of an accounting firm differ greatly from those of a football team. Accountants devote hours on end to researching changes in the tax code and reviewing financial documents. They must be able to work independently, focus for long periods of time, and analyze every detail of the material they are reading.

A football team member also puts in long hours at work. Instead of reading accounting journals, a player spends hours on the field practicing and learning new plays and strategies. A player must be able to concentrate on the flow of the game, the position of teammates and opponents, the score, and time left to play, as well as be flexible enough to create new plays on the fly and recover from stumbles. Sounds like the perfect employee to drive your organization to success, right? Not so fast.

If I had an apple for every manager who told me he wanted to hire someone because he'd mastered a particular sport, I would have a thriving orchard. I'm not saying these people should not be hired, but rather that there are many other factors to consider before awarding these candidates a place on your team.

Being a first-rate accountant or an excellent football player requires particular knowledge, skills, abilities, and personal characteristics. The same is true for being an excellent employee in any organization.

When selecting new employees, you must look for individuals who have a blend of knowledge, skills, abilities, and personal characteristics that will enable them to best perform the required activities of the job. While the company may help new employees develop some of the skills required, people must bring certain characteristics to the position if they are going to succeed in their respective roles in a particular company.

The most successful employees are: people who enjoy coming to work every day, the ones other people like working with, and those who do their jobs well. They possess personal characteristics that are critical for success in most work environments. We also refer to these personal characteristics as behaviors, or traits. They can be grouped into three categories with regard to their orientation toward:

1. **Work and other activities.** This is how an employee performs—not just the work that he does. Included in this category are: sense of urgency; a "do it now" attitude; customer focus (he goes above and beyond to delight the customer); initiative (he

sees something that needs to be done and does it without prompting); and enthusiasm, eagerness, and excitement.

2. **Others.** Most businesses entail working with other employees and with customers. The most successful employees possess solid interpersonal skills and can work well in groups as well as independently. This category includes: friendliness (she enjoys spending time with other people and demonstrates a pleasant demeanor) and team orientation (she demonstrates a willingness to work with others toward shared goals).

3. **Themselves.** It is important for employees to present themselves appropriately and to be capable of managing the physical and emotional demands of the job. This category includes: innovation (he is willing to take chances and think out of the box); image consciousness (he pays careful attention to his personal appearance, dress, and speech); and fitness (he possesses the requisite stamina).

There are additional traits that we seek when hiring managers and salespeople, as both these jobs require a unique set of characteristics for long-term success. Taking the time to define the traits that are most important to your organization can prevent you from wasting hundreds of hours interviewing people who, if hired, will never fit into your organization, nor would they succeed.

Can You Really Change Behavior?

Some executives hire for skill and then hire psychologists to help them try to change people's behavior. In fact, I recently spoke with a CEO who has one of his key people in therapy now. I suspect this employee will never get off the couch. This approach is similar to hiring a contractor with a reputation for rarely showing up and then expecting him to be on the job site daily. Dreams do come true, but only if you are living in Disneyland.

I believe there are enough good people out there with the characteristics you are seeking. Hire them and, if need be, invest in training to improve their skills. You'll have much more success with this approach than the one where you try to turn someone into something she'll never be.

Roy Ng of SAP is very much in tune with this philosophy. "I'm all about the fit, the passion, and the ability to learn. I want someone who can think freshly about any topic," states Ng. Ng, who used to work for Goldman Sachs, recalls having stacks of résumés on his desk from candidates who went to top schools and had top grades. "In the end, the paper only tells you so much. I'd trade some of the paper achievement for some of the intangibles. You can't judge the book by its cover, but the fit piece is pretty critical."

Three Major Components of the Magnetic Interviewing Process

The magnetic interviewing process can be broken down into three major components: eliciting behavior, observing behavior, and interpreting behavior. A clear understanding of each of these components will enable you to improve your hiring success exponentially.

Eliciting Behavior

In order to elicit natural behavior from candidates, you must be able to put candidates at ease. This will result in answers that are more honest and reflective of the candidate. Setting the stage for the interview should be given more than just a moment's thought. I've had clients tell me that they've deliberately interviewed candidates in places like bars and airports to see how they operate with distractions all around them. I can understand why my clients in the beer industry find this setting to be appropriate, given that the salespeople they hire are meeting with customers under similar conditions, but it makes absolutely no sense if you are trying to hire a librarian.

Find a quiet place to conduct your first round of interviews, even if that means that you need to borrow a conference room so you have some privacy. Always remember to turn your cell phone off and place your office phone on "do not disturb," so that you can give your full attention to the person who has taken the time out of his day to meet with you. When in doubt, treat others as you would like to be treated.

Interviewers are often unaware of how the tone of their voice comes across to candidates. A warm, interested, conversational tone throughout the interview really helps elicit natural behavior from others. It's no coincidence that therapists take this approach with their patients, as it allows them to gain trust more rapidly. Imagine if a therapist came across as harsh and judgmental. The patient would likely share very little. Yet this is exactly the way some interviewers sound in interviews as they probe more deeply into areas that may hit close to a nerve. I can tell you from personal experience that when a candidate feels comfortable, she will tell you way more than you want to know, and, quite frankly, sometimes the information revealed can save you months of trying to figure out how to release this person from your organization. Be aware of your tone, remain nonjudgmental, and take notes on your observations.

Another way to elicit telling behavior from a candidate is to use open-ended questions. These are questions that cannot be answered with a yes or a no. For example, rather than asking, "Did you enjoy the work that you did at your last job?" you would instead say, "Describe for me what you enjoyed most and least about the work you did at your last job." Of course, there will be times when you will be across the desk from someone who is a bit too succinct. He may give you a very brief answer. A good way to keep the conversation going, while still keeping the candidate at ease, is to use phrases like, "Really? Tell me more" and "And then what happened?"

Observing Behavior

This is the second component of the magnetic interviewing process, and one that is particularly difficult for CEOs and senior executives to do properly, as many are focused on "results" and are quick to make judgments. It's important to understand that it takes time for candidates to relax. A candidate's behavior at the beginning of the interview may be more a matter of nerves than an accurate reflection of who he truly is. It's only natural, after having made a decision about a person, that you keep looking for subsequent data to confirm your decision. To avoid this pitfall, interviewers must push themselves to continually and objectively observe the immediate behavior of the applicant and to take comprehensive notes.

How applicants present themselves throughout the course of the interview is much more important than what they say. For example, an applicant who says, "I was the most productive salesperson in the company," and delivers this statement in a slow, monotonous manner, should cause you to take note. If I were conducting the interview, I'd be thinking, "If this guy was truly the best, how bad was everyone else?" It's important to note how responses are delivered, rather than what is said. It is all too easy to be razzled and dazzled by words, especially when interviewing salespeople who are masters of storytelling. In a situation like this, I'd recommend jotting down a note on your pad that says, "Claimed productivity—showed no energy or enthusiasm."

Throughout the interview, note everything the applicant does. Record observed behavior, not what you think is going on inside the person's mind. Record subtle changes in behavior during the interview as well as the context of the change (e.g., "when discussing her previous supervisor or when asked why she left her last job, applicant seemed to squirm and was hesitant before responding"). Place a check mark by a noted behavior each time you see it. This will help you better track patterns.

Interpreting Behavior

This is best done after the interview has been completed and the applicant has left the room. Look closely at your notes and highlight those patterns of behavior that you observed three or more times throughout the interview. Match the behavior observed to the reported facts and your own observation. When there appears to be a conflict between what the candidate said and what you observed, base your opinions on what you saw. Lastly, but most importantly, be hypercritical. An applicant tries to put his best foot forward in an interview. What you saw was the candidate at his best. Ask yourself, "Is this good enough?"

You'll also dramatically improve your ability to select the right people for your organization if you go into the interview with prepared questions. It's okay to look down at your list of questions, so don't feel like you have to memorize them. It's also okay, and in fact highly recommended, that you take notes throughout the process. As many of you know already, if you are interviewing many candidates they may begin to blend together, and it may become difficult to recall exactly who said what.

You also might want to take a play from the handbook of Humana's Paul Kraemer. Kraemer makes it a point to take candidates to lunch or dinner:

> "You can tell a great deal from the way a candidate interacts with a hostess or the waiter. Our business is a service business, which means communication skills are extremely important. You can sit in an office all day with a candidate and you may never get a good sense of what they are like when they are relaxed and around other people. Or you can take an hour out of your day to do lunch and see them in action."

Pass the bread, please!

Interviewing Errors and How to Avoid Them

I've conducted numerous interviews and have trained hundreds of managers on how to interview; following are some of the common interviewing errors I've observed.

1. **Leaping to conclusions.** Interviewers often draw conclusions about candidates' abilities on the basis of insufficient or invalid information. It's impossible to conclude anything about a person from a single piece of information. For example, you cannot conclude that an applicant who is neatly dressed and well groomed will do meticulous work. Similarly, because an applicant was a track star, you cannot conclude that this individual will be competitive in a work environment. In both cases, you need more information. If you look at patterns of behavior, you are likelier to reach a more valid conclusion.

2. **Talking too much.** This is by far the most common interviewing error. When interviewers do the majority

of the talking, they cannot possibly do an effective job of eliciting and observing the candidate's behavior. And, of course, they cannot accurately evaluate the candidate, as they know little about this person in spite of the fact that they may have spent an entire hour together. Most interviewers who talk too much do so out of anxiety or a lack of understanding of how to conduct an interview. Through practice and a clear understanding of the process, you should be able to steer clear of this common error.

3. **Shutting down candidates before they open up.** By its nature, the interview situation makes most applicants somewhat tense. If the person doing the interviewing is cold, distant, or argumentative, applicants will shut down and reveal little about themselves, which is unfortunate if the person appears to have been a perfect fit for the job.

4. **Succumbing to the halo effect.** I usually cringe when I'm observing an interview and the person doing the interviewing realizes that he and the candidate pledged the same fraternity at the same college. Immediately, the interviewer assumes that "if we both were in the same fraternity and we attended the same school, we are both exceptional!" This is what we call the halo effect, and you must be alert and guard against it. A wide spectrum of students attended that same college, and most likely all were not exceptional, even if that college was Harvard.

5. **Leading the witness.** This is where you begin the question by telling the candidate what you want to hear: "You know, being a small business, we don't have a lot of administrative support available. That means we all have to pitch in. How do you think you'd

fit into a company like ours since your background is mostly Fortune 500 companies?" Of course, any decent candidate will tell you exactly what you want to hear: "I'm used to pitching in wherever needed. I'll do whatever it takes."

6. **Being too lenient.** Most people want to think well of others. Unfortunately, this tendency can get in the way of seeing people for who they really are. Your job as the interviewer is to make sure that you hire the best person for the job. It is not anyone's interest to place applicants in positions where they ultimately will fail.

Common Selection Mistakes

There are numerous selection mistakes that can easily be avoided. Here are five of the most common mistakes, along with tips to help you sidestep them.

1. Failure to Clearly Define the Role

Have you ever walked into a store like Costco without a list in hand? I have—$300 and a cart full of everything but what I really needed is usually the result of this lunatic move. Hiring managers make this same costly mistake all the time. They fail to clearly define what it is they are looking for, so they keep going up and down the aisles, throwing candidates into their shopping carts in the hope that one will be exactly what they need.

What if, instead, you took the time to clearly define what it is this person will be doing and the traits or behaviors you are seeking before entering the big box sites like Career-Builder or Monster? You'll certainly have fewer people in your cart, but you also won't be spending excess dollars talking with people who may or may not have what you are looking for—and even you don't know what that is.

2. Failure to Cast a Wide Net

Posting a job on your website or on Craigslist isn't exactly what I would call thinking big, especially if no one has ever heard of your company. I tell job seekers they should use every avenue available to let others know they are looking for employment, and I'm offering you the same advice as well. There will be occasions where casting your net wider may make more sense than taking a targeted approach to recruiting. For example, suppose you are opening up a new facility and you need to swiftly hire people for the grand opening. In these situations, having a large pool of qualified candidates will serve you well. The key word here is *qualified*.

If you cast your net wide and you catch a few people who shouldn't be in there, it's easy to release them back into the candidate pool. It's much harder to do this when you only have a few people on the end of your line. Instead of releasing them, business owners and hiring managers convince themselves that they are better off having a body in the job than leaving the position vacant. Every hire represents your company. Think about that before you decide it's okay to insert a warm body in your organization as a placeholder.

Here's a checklist to help you increase your magnetic pull when looking to attract top talent. Choose the item(s) that are most appropriate given the position you are hiring for, the number of vacancies you are trying to fill, and the state of the job market in your area.

- ☐ Company website
- ☐ Internal company newsletter
- ☐ Client newsletter (if appropriate)
- ☐ Employee referrals
- ☐ Friends

☐ LinkedIn

☐ Facebook fan page

☐ Personal Facebook page

☐ Twitter (several times a week)

☐ Pinterest

☐ Other social media platforms

☐ Place of worship

☐ College placement office

☐ Alumni placement office

☐ CEO group

☐ City websites

☐ Associations

☐ Chamber of commerce

☐ Newspapers

☐ Job boards

☐ Temp agencies

☐ Government agencies

☐ Third-party recruiter

☐ Search firm

☐ Other (which may or may not exist as of this writing!)

3. Refusal to Pay Recruitment Fees

It's great if you are in the fortunate position of not having to pay recruitment fees, but most organizations aren't this lucky, especially if they are trying to fill key positions in parts of the country or around the globe that are far from headquarters. I've known several organizations that have proudly flaunted the fact that they never pay agency fees. These are the same companies that keep posting what appear to be the same jobs over and over again.

Whether you pay recruitment fees should really come down to available time and dollars and "sense," instead of pride. If you can fill a job with the right candidate on your own, then I say do it. If you are unable to do so or you have other pressing matters, then use a third-party recruiter or a contract recruiter who will dedicate herself to searching and bringing in talent exclusively for your organization.

4. Hiring for Skills Rather Than Fit

You can train for skill. You cannot train for fit. If you have to choose between one or the other, and it's not a matter of life or death, (e.g., a surgeon), always go with fit. Every CEO and executive I interviewed for this book said the same thing. If you hire smart people whose values are aligned with those of the organization, you can teach them what they need to know.

If you honestly believe that you are going to teach a thirty-year-old to play nice in the sandbox, then I suggest you spend a few days working at a day-care center, where you can observe professional day-care workers teaching young children how to be nice to one another. Most are unable to accomplish this on the first, second, or even third try. What makes you think you'll be more successful?

5. Hiring Mr. Right for Right Now

I know dozens of women who settled for Mr. Right for right now, and I can tell you that, in the end, all had regrets. Here's where patience pays off. Ignore all those people who are telling you that you are being too picky, especially if those people will be receiving hefty checks if you hire one of their candidates. Instead, be patient.

I know there were times throughout my career where I would have done anything to get a position filled. One time in particular comes to mind. In my first job out of college, I worked for a retailer called Foleys, which is now part of the Macy's family. I worked in the flagship store in downtown Houston. I was responsible for hiring the store's Santa Claus, an important yet difficult position to fill, especially given the requirements of the job and the pay scale. I just about jumped into the lap of the first guy who looked like he had what it took to fit the uniform. In retrospect, I should have been more patient. Do you know how difficult it is to replace a Santa Claus in early December when all the good candidates are busy overseeing elves in other stores? Don't even get me started about my experiences hiring the Easter Bunny!

Cutting the Interview Short
When There Is No Spark

We've all been there. You are sitting across the table interviewing someone who clearly isn't the right fit. Some people believe it's only polite to continue the interview and give the person the full amount of time that has been set aside. I believe this is neither fair to the candidate nor a good use of your time. What if, instead, you were completely honest with the person you were meeting with? This way, they don't leave thinking they have a shot at the job when they don't.

Here's the language for cutting the interview short that I share with those who attend my workshops on Selecting for Success: "It's clear to me that this isn't really the right fit. Rather than waste your time, I believe it's best to end here." If I truly believe the candidate is great and I know of a position elsewhere that would be a better fit, I ask for permission to forward the applicant's résumé to my contact at the other company. Most people graciously agree and thank me for doing so.

The Art of Reference Checking

One of the first questions I ask my clients when a new hire doesn't work out is whether there were any red flags during the reference-checking process. I usually receive a blank stare followed by some babbling about not checking references or making an offer after only one attempt to contact a reference. Not checking references is a lot like choosing not to vote. If you aren't going to bother, then you don't get to complain when you don't like the outcome.

The problem with most reference-checking processes is that they are merely concerned with checking off a series of boxes and, in some cases, I mean this literally. I received an e-mail the other day from a colleague informing me that I would be receiving a request for a reference check from an automated system. This request was coming from a major hospital where he was applying for a fairly senior-level position. I have to say, I was a bit taken back that such an important matter would be left to automation. I did what I suspect everyone else did. I quickly read through the questions, checked all "5s" for outstanding, filled in a few blanks, and went on my merry way. The whole time I was thinking, "Why bother?" What do they really expect to learn about a candidate with this process? Nothing, is my guess.

Who to Call for References and Who to Avoid

When checking references, always try to speak directly with the person the candidate has worked for. You can avoid hearing this person say that company policy doesn't permit her to give out references by asking the candidate to contact the person ahead of time to let her know you'll be calling for a reference. If you are thinking this is a mistake, as the candidate will prep the person giving the reference, I can assure you that the applicant will do this anyway.

Here's who you don't want to talk with:

- ℭ Coworkers, as most won't have direct knowledge of the candidate's skills or level of expertise.
- ℭ HR, whose job it is to protect the company from defamation suits. They will only give out name, title, and dates of employment.
- ℭ The candidate's mom, who in most cases will give a glowing review!

Reference Questions That Will Help You Cut to the Chase

Your objective when checking references is to confirm what you believe to be true and to determine areas where edges may need to be smoothed. Having this information in hand will allow you to make a more informed hiring decision.

The Million-Dollar Reference-Checking Question

No matter the position you are hiring for, the following is my all-time favorite question:

On a scale of one to ten, with ten being the highest, how would you rate the overall performance of _____? If the response given is less than a ten (which it usually is), follow up with: What would it take for you to rate this person a ten? Now we're talking, as you now know those areas where improvement may be needed. Follow up by asking the person to expand on what he just said.

The questions that you should be asking will depend on the job requirements and the level of the position you are hiring for. For example, you most certainly will want to ask a former manager to describe how an applicant handled irate customers if the position you are hiring for requires strong customer service skills. You'd want to ask more detailed questions related to this topic if this person was going to be heading up your customer service operations.

What to Do with a Negative Reference

I'll be the first to admit that we really want references to check out as we had hoped, because we usually only check them when we are fairly certain we'd like to extend an offer. If you do enough reference checks, eventually you'll come across some negative references. While you don't want to discount entirely what you are being told, you do have to consider the source. For example, a colleague of mine was just fired from her firm because her boss told her he was "uncomfortable with her success outside of work." You see, she had recently had a book published. He then went on to say that he couldn't get past the fact that she didn't ask him to cowrite the book. One can only imagine what he will be saying when people call him for a reference about this employee. If the majority of references are telling you one thing and someone tells you something entirely different, then you may want to go ahead and take a chance with this person.

If you do receive negative feedback about a potential employee, you can certainly confirm this with the next reference by asking specific questions to help you determine if what you are being told is a consistent problem or a situation that occurred early on in the candidate's career and hasn't happened since.

Rule of Attraction

Every hiring manager and anyone involved in the hiring process should have the skills to assess talent. Go to *www.matusonconsulting.com* to download a copy of *Selecting for Success: The Complete Guide to Hiring Top Talent.*

CHAPTER

Retention Matters

What's the point of pulling in great talent if you can't keep them in your employ? I know a number of companies that are revolving doors, with people exiting as fast as they are entering. One can get dizzy watching this parade in motion.

Business owners and executives are far too busy paying attention to the revenue side of the business, and as a result they lose sight of what really matters—the relationships that drive their business. People do businesses with people, not companies. When workers leave your employ, they take their relationships with them. This is true whether they are working on the front line or on the back end of the business. They are also sharing what they really think about your firm (both good and bad) through their social media networks for all to see.

I have followed my favorite hairdresser wherever she has gone, even if it meant more than an hour's drive for me. We all have personal relationships with the repair people who come into our homes (sometimes more often than we care to remember). I honestly couldn't tell you the company the repair people I use work for because I only know their names and their cell phone numbers. I can only imagine the loss of revenue and reputation that occurs when good employees leave businesses that rely on word of mouth for their daily bread.

The High Cost of Employee Turnover

I believe CEOs and senior executives don't pay much attention to employee turnover because they don't have a full understanding of what turnover really costs an organization. That's because somewhere along the line, in an effort to simplify life, someone came up with a nice, compact formula that fit perfectly into a package, and others bought it. I'm talking about the one times, two times, or three times annual earnings formula that people use to calculate the cost of turnover.

Here is a perfect example of why this formula is more harmful than good. According to Salary.com, the median salary for a receptionist in Boston, Massachusetts, is $32,955. If you subscribe to the accepter turnover-cost formulas, this means that the loss of a receptionist will cost your firm either $32,955, $65,910, or $98,865. These numbers appear to be far from reality, but you won't know unless you actually do the math. Not to mention that there is a huge gap between the low end of the spectrum and the high end. You might as well throw a dart at a chart full of numbers and pick whichever one you hit. No wonder CEOs and other senior executives shake their heads and ignore conversations when the cost of employee turnover is mentioned.

CEOs are generally bright people who are good with numbers. They read articles in business publications that repeat these ridiculous formulas and quickly discount them. I'm glad they do. However, the conversation still needs to be had. Here's why.

Lost Knowledge

When an employee leaves an organization, he takes with him the knowledge he has, including knowledge specific to the organization. This is often referred to as institutional knowledge. It can be as simple as being the only one who knows how to fix a particular thorny problem or it can be more complex, like knowing the history of and rationale behind certain business decisions and how they play into the future viability of the organization.

In some situations, it can take years to replace the knowledge that goes out the door when an employee leaves. Sometimes this knowledge can be brought in from the outside. A consultant may be able to bridge the knowledge gap, but this is usually a temporary fix and can be costly over the long term. Ask yourself, "What's the cost of losing this knowledge? What can I do today to prevent it from happening?"

Disruption of the Team

It takes time for a team to become fully productive, and in some cases this never occurs because team members are swapped out before the group has hit its stride. When teams are operating properly, work is assigned to ensure everyone is pulling her weight. When one member leaves the team, the weight gets redistributed, and time lines must be adjusted. Imagine the impact employee turnover has on a team that is responsible for the development of new products. That may explain why some products are obsolete before they ever make it out the door.

Loss of Reputation

In highly competitive industries like hospitality, reputation truly differentiates one hotel from another. Without the edge a stellar reputation bestows, you are merely another building with beds. Niki Leondakis, CEO of San Francisco–based Commune Hotels & Resorts and former president and COO of Kimpton Hotels, is mindful of the impact employee turnover can have on business. "When you have longevity in your workforce, that's when you really start to see consistency and harmony," explains Leondakis. The opposite is true when you don't have a steady workforce. Customers who are expecting one thing and wind up with something that isn't up to the usual standards quickly shy away from that hotel, vowing never to return.

Recently I attended an event at the W Hotel in Times Square. For years, the W brand had a reputation of really slick hotels that were operated at a level far above that of their competitors. People didn't hesitate to pay the extra required to book at one of these hotels because they knew the experience would be consistently worth it. Not so much anymore. Friends who stayed at this hotel told tales of dirty room-service dishes remaining outside rooms well into the early morning. They complained of poor service when filing complaints that are too nasty to describe here. Clearly, the reputation of this hotel and, consequently, the W brand, has slid. With a hotel on almost every corner in NYC, travelers can be picky about where they lay their heads at night. With high employee turnover comes an influx of new staff members, many of whom are not properly trained before they are tossed out on the floor. Without a solid reputation, what do you have?

Increased Difficulty Attracting People

We all know of companies that we've been advised to stay away from when seeking new employment opportunities. Phrases like "They'll chew you up and spit you out" and "You'll sell yourself to the devil if you go to work for them" are some of the nicer things being said about these organizations.

Of course, some desperate people do go to work for these companies. How do I know this? Because their actions let us know every day that they'd much rather be someplace else.

Turnover at Kimpton Hotels is quite low, and Kimpton is now experiencing the benefits of having staff who really want to work for their company. "Being able to fill open positions quickly with top talent allows you to not miss a beat," states Niki Leondakis. "You may only get what the agency finds if you aren't pulling in your own talent." Leondakis goes on to talk about her recent experience hiring a chief information officer. "Within two weeks of announcing the opening, I had 250 highly qualified applicants and I didn't have to go through a search firm." Leondakis would not have been so fortunate if her company had had the reputation of a workplace where few want to be. Hence, you can see that it makes both dollars and "sense" to control employee turnover.

Employee Turnover in Terms of Products and Services

Estimates of turnover costs for a single position range from 30 percent of the yearly salary for hourly employees to 150 percent, as estimated by the Saratoga Institute. The McQuaig Institute puts this into terms that most of us can relate to: a fast-food restaurant must sell 7,613 children's combo meals at $2.50 each to recoup the cost of losing just one crew member. To recoup the cost of losing just one sales clerk, a clothing store must sell almost 3,000 pairs of khakis at $35. How many of your products or services must you sell to make up for the loss of one employee?

Your Real Cost of Employee Turnover

We've established that many companies rely on data produced from mystical formulas that are merely smoke and mirrors and that obscure the real cost of employee turnover.

Some may argue that these formulas are better than nothing. I disagree. You may as well pluck a number out of the sky—your guess will be as good, if not better, than one produced by using these formulas. So how do you calculate the real cost of employee turnover? Warning: the following diagnostic tool will help you come up with a number that, for many, will be shocking. But isn't it better to know the true cost of employee turnover, so you can better assess the ROI of programs you may be considering to help you reduce this number?

Many companies are still fat and happy. Like waistlines all across the globe, employee turnover is expanding at an alarming rate. Yet companies are still following the same regimen, hoping to control their expanding costs. Nobody, including me, wants to step on the scale and face reality, especially if it's been a while since you've stood naked in front of the mirror. How much money are you wasting on satisfying short-term needs? Taking shortcuts may give you immediate satisfaction, but they will hurt you in the end. If you knew you could shave hundreds of thousands of dollars off your recruitment and hiring costs while adding millions to your bottom line, would you be willing to address the issues that are slowing your company down and, in some cases, making it impossible to move toward healthier profits? Like losing weight, it can be painful to take that first step. But once you do, you will feel empowered, knowing that you are one step closer to getting your organization back into shape. Let's begin.

Create a list of everyone who has left your organization this year. If you want to capture a full year's worth of information, consider obtaining the data for those who left the company the previous year as well. The business costs and impact of employee turnover can be grouped into four major categories:

1. Costs due to a person leaving
2. Hiring costs
3. Training costs
4. Lost productivity costs

Costs Due to a Person Leaving

Employees who have announced their resignation have already begun to transition out of the company. While working out their notice period, their full attention is no longer on your business. Others in the organization are picking up their slack, which prohibits them from giving full attention to their own jobs. In addition, consider the following costs and jot down your answers in the right hand column, or if you prefer, go to www.matusonconsulting.com to access our free online employee turnover calculator:

Situation	Actual Cost
Cost of employees who must fill in for the person who leaves before a replacement is found	
Payments for temporary help or consultants to fill in while position is re-staffed	
The cost of the time spent by manager or executive for exit interview with the employee to determine what work remains, how to do work, why employee is leaving	
The amount of money the company has invested in the departing person's training; the cost of lost knowledge, skills, and contacts that will depart with employee	
Cost of lost customers the departing employee is taking with her (or who will leave because service is negatively impacted)	
The increased cost of unemployment insurance	
Separation pay	
Subtotal	$

Hiring Costs

You might get lucky and find a candidate on a free website, but most likely you'll need to post and advertise elsewhere. Consider the following hiring costs:

Situation	Actual Cost
The cost of advertising, Internet postings, employment agencies, search firms, employee referral awards	
Increase in starting pay, as salaries have risen since you last hired, adjusting everyone else in the department's pay to ensure parity	
The cost of time spent screening résumés, arranging interviews, conducting interviews (by both HR and upper management), checking references, and notifying candidates who were not awarded the job	
Fees associated with assessment testing, background checks, drug screening (usually done on more than one candidate), and time spent interpreting and discussing results	
Cost of time spent assembling and processing new-hire paperwork, explaining employee benefit programs, and entering data to ensure employee receives a paycheck	
Subtotal	$

Training Costs

It would be great if all employees arrived fully assembled, but this is not usually the case. Things are done differently in every organization, so you must factor in the following costs:

Situation	Actual Cost
Cost of new employee orientation or onboarding	
Money allotted for training for the person to perform his job, such as computer training, product knowledge, company systems, leadership courses	
Cost of time spent by others to train this person	
Subtotal	$

Loss of Productivity Costs

Because new employees do not enter an organization fully trained, it will take time before they are fully productive. Factor in the following productivity costs:

Situation	Actual Cost
Cost of time the manager is spending directing, reviewing work, and possibly fixing mistakes	
Outlay for errors that were not caught by manager	
Cost associated with loss of good will as you scramble to preserve your relationship with valued customers and clients	
Loss from plummeting employee morale as overworked employees assume more responsibility while the new hire is being trained	
Cost of turning away new business as you continue to focus on stabilizing your company.	
Subtotal	$

Tally up your subtotals to determine the full cost of losing an employee.

Categories Associated with Turnover Costs	Subtotals of Actual Costs
Costs due to a person leaving	
Hiring costs	
Training costs	
Loss of productivity costs	
Total cost	$

Note: Go to www.matusonconsulting.com to access my *free* online employee turnover calculator, which will automatically tally these numbers for you.

Now, rinse and repeat this formula or multiply according to the number of incumbents who have left this position. Plug this information into a spreadsheet to determine the real cost of employee turnover in your organization. How do you measure up? Are you in better shape than you thought, or is it time for an intervention?

As you can see for yourself, employee turnover can dramatically impact productivity, customer retention, and your bottom line. Paying even a small bit of attention to this matter can make a big difference. As you read on, consider that employee turnover is a lot like eating a piece of dark chocolate. In moderation, both are fine and can even be healthy, which we'll discuss later in this book (healthy employee turnover, not dark chocolate). In excess, both can have serious ramifications.

Capturing the Hearts of Employees: Principles of Employee Retention

Companies are spending billions of dollars trying to help employees with work–life balance, but many of these efforts are not achieving the desired result. Here's what one of my clients did instead.

> We never quite understood the need for formalized work/life balance programs. That's because at UM International, we believe in living one whole life. There may be days when we are burning the midnight oil and other times when we are riding off into the sunset on our motorcycles. We measure people on results, not face time, and we provide team members with the flexibility and resources they need to live one glorious life.

Many people leave organizations because they feel they have to choose between work and family. Companies like UM International make it easy for employees to stay, because they don't have to choose between work and life.

There are a number of companies where CEOs are improving conditions for employees because they want to, not because they have to, and this is having a positive impact on morale and employee retention. Chris Knight, CEO of SparkNET, is one of these CEOs.

Magnetic Leader Chris Knight

Chris Knight, CEO of SparkNET—a high-tech Internet firm and mobile app development company based in Green Bay, Wisconsin—spent the past two years designing and building a new facility for his employees and *with* his employees, as quite a few of the team members were involved in the decision making. "We make decisions that make no economic sense at all because we believe it's important for people to love being in the space they are in. I want people to feel like work is as fun as being at home," Knight says. For example, "The staff wanted window space. They wanted to see the outside world from their workspace. It was really important to them, so we added more windows than originally planned," explains Knight.

There is a sundeck on the second floor and plenty of outdoor spaces for staff to eat or grab some sunshine in the afternoon. The state-of-the-art fitness center was built to help his people recharge and reset their brains. Of course, a workplace wouldn't be like home without a thermal spa, so Knight threw one of those in as well. There's also a gourmet kitchen, where a chef prepares free, healthy, and delicious meals for SparkNET employees.

Knight jokes about being located in the Silicon Cheese Valley, since his company is in Green Bay, Wisconsin. He wanted to have a campfire area inside the building where his employees could gather, but he had to give up on that idea due to permitting issues.

"I'm doing these things because I want to, not because I have to," notes Knight. "I want to have fun at work. I want to have no regrets at the end of my life. I believe the purpose of life is to provide value to others." And indeed, Knight is doing that. Knight has also significantly reduced the stress that is often associated with turnover because his turnover rate is low—in the low single digits. He adds, "I have a young team and we all know they won't be there for life. We'll have fun for now."

Making a commitment to your employees' well-being is another way of capturing the hearts of your employees.

Magnetic Leader Tom Kulzer

Tom Kulzer is CEO and founder of AWeber Communications, located in Chalfont, Pennsylvania. The company develops and manages opt-in e-mail marketing tools. Kulzer is proud of the fact that the company pays 100 percent of the health-care premiums for his employees, whose average age is twenty-eight. "From a retention point, this may not seem important to the team now, but as they age and their personal situations change, they will value this more." Kulzer also provides daily catered lunches to all employees: "The employees select what they want and we have it delivered."

Kulzer is building a new facility, which will have an on-site kitchen. There, chefs will come in and prepare meals for the employees. Currently, everyone piles into the lunchroom and plays card games, or they can go to the theater room where they can watch a movie. "The more they do together, the more cohesive the team becomes." Kulzer goes on to say, "When you are friends with the people you work with, you are less likely to leave. People look forward to coming to work to be with their friends."

Magnetic Leader Ed Kushins

Ed Kushins, founder and CEO of HomeExchange.com, based in Hermosa, California, is someone who regularly invites people into his home, including the gentleman who eventually became a business partner. Kushins knew his neighbor was doing a home exchange, so he invited his neighbor's guest over for a barbecue. The rest, as they say, is history. The company has quickly grown to become one of the United States's largest members-only home exchange businesses. Here is what Kushins does to ensure his employees feel at home when they are at work.

(continues)

"I've brought on a few people without having a specific spot for them. If someone really wants to contribute to HomeExchange, I'll find them a spot," says Kushins. Everyone in Kushins's organization is passionate about the HomeExchange experience. Kushins makes it a point to give people the opportunity to work in areas where they seem to shine. When someone maxes out, he gives that person permission to hire another person so the employee is free to take on more challenging work. "We trust the judgment of the people we hire," says Kushins.

Once a year, Kushins brings the entire team and their families together, and he has done so for years. "The team is now becoming friends with everyone and not just business associates. Everyone brings their families to our annual meeting." In case you are interested, the next meeting will be held in Sicily!

Kushins works hard to make sure his people understand how important the work they do is to HomeExchange.com. Every day, he builds on what he calls a culture of excitement to make sure the company remains an interesting and exciting place to be. "They know I love our team, and I really acknowledge and appreciate everything our people are doing for us," Kushins explains. Thanks to technology, he is able to do this daily, no matter where in the world he happens to be that day.

Future Shock

In the future, workplace longevity may very well be measured in months rather than years. The sooner you accept this possibility, the better prepared you will be for the future state of the employment relationship.

All of the magnetic leaders I interviewed for this book acknowledged that most talent cannot be held onto forever. You have to embrace the possibility that at any moment, another employee will take flight from your company's departure lounge. Niki Leondakis, CEO of Commune Hotels

& Resorts, understands this on both an emotional and a business level. When it comes to her employees, she says, "I hope you stay with us forever. We understand that life takes its turns, and when you do leave, we hope you come back." Leondakis's former employer, Kimpton, welcomes former employees back with open arms—a strategy that will serve them well as predicted labor shortages become reality.

Knight also understands this. "I have a young team, and we all know they won't be with us for life. We'll have fun for now."

You can prepare for the future now by:

- Encouraging people to leave the nest when they show signs of restlessness.
- Welcoming returning employees back into the fold.
- Reviewing policies and adjusting accordingly so rehires don't have to start their employee benefits clock all over again.
- Staying connected with former employees and encouraging them to recommend you to job seekers.
- Always being on the lookout for great talent.

Rule of Attraction

Complete the diagnostic tool (or do so online at www.matusonconsulting.com) to determine the real cost of employee turnover in your organization. Then calculate how much in products or services you must sell to make up for the loss of one employee. Have I gotten your attention yet?

Warning Signs You May Be Losing Your Magnetic Touch

You can tell a lot about an organization by the feeling you get when you walk in the door. The overall tone of the business often reflects the state of employee morale, which is defined by Businessdirectory.com as the emotions, attitude, satisfaction, and overall outlook of employees during their time in a workplace environment. Employee morale varies considerably from organization to organization and can fluctuate from one department to another within the same organization.

Gallup and others have conducted extensive research on the impact workplace morale has on employee engagement. It's extremely difficult, if not impossible, to be fully engaged when you are operating in a sea of cubicles where everyone is drowning in misery. You can only tread for so long until eventually you tire and either jump into the same boat as those around you or abandon ship.

Those who are fortunate enough to work in businesses where morale is high generally feel good about their work.

These employees are often referred to as highly engaged. This type of magnetism pays off substantially. They are willing to go above and beyond the call of duty on behalf of their employers. According to Gallup, highly engaged employees are more productive and profitable, provide high levels of customer service, and are less likely to leave the company when tempted by generous offers from other firms. Organizations with highly engaged workforces are generally more profitable than those with workforces that consist of people who are moderately engaged or disengaged.

The Silent Killer: Employee Quietness

I recently had several meetings with a prospect, and each time I visited their offices I left with a feeling that all was not right with this organization. The office, which consisted of mostly young employees sitting in clusters of cubicles, was alarmingly quiet. I've never been in an office with a young staff and deafening silence. There were no sounds of laughter, nor were there any conversations by the water cooler. This may not have caught my attention had it been a stodgy law firm or a financial company on Wall Street. But this was a technology company. I left wondering (well, I sort of knew) how employee morale was in that organization, and whether anyone else realized or cared that there could be a problem.

I couldn't help but think about Opower, which has a similar demographic. I recently watched a YouTube video of a flash mob Opower's employees did to the song "Call Me Maybe," a clip the company proudly includes on its website. Even before the video begins, you can hear chatter and the sound of laughter coming from the office cubicles. I thought to myself, "Wow! These two companies couldn't be more different, and if I had offers from each of these organizations, I'd choose Opower."

I've had the opportunity to speak with the CEOs of both of these companies, and they are as different as night and day. When Opower's CEO, Dan Yates, speaks about his people, you can feel his enthusiasm. So much so, that I actually thought about hopping a plane and going to work for him. The other CEO? Let's just say I was relieved when I found out that a friend's daughter didn't make it through the hiring process. She was an outstanding candidate who deserved to be in a workplace where her brilliant personality could shine. I'm happy to say that she eventually found such a place. I have no doubt which company will be making lots of noise for years to come and which will disappear quietly into the night.

It's certainly harder for a CEO or other senior executive to have her finger on the pulse of the organization when she is part of the landscape or, in some cases, part of the problem. But if you are open and you listen deeply, you will be able to identify the warning signs that clearly indicate you may be losing your magnetic touch.

Thankfully, there are tools to help leaders measure employee happiness and employee engagement. Here's one for your use.

Take the following Employee Retention Self-Assessment to see how you fare in terms of employee retention. Consider having your management team complete this self-assessment and asking their team members to do the same. Compare the results and focus on any areas where there appears to be a huge disconnect between what you believe to be true and what others believe to be true.

Note: It's certainly best to have an outside person administer the assessment, as employees are generally more honest when they are 100 percent sure their answers will be anonymous. However, if you are confident that your organization has high levels of trust, then doing this on your own may yield the information you need to identify and address gaps.

EMPLOYEE RETENTION SELF-ASSESSMENT

Please rate your company according to each of the following statements:	Ratings
	4 = All the time 3 = Most of the time 2 = Sometimes 1 = Rarely 0 = Never N/A = Not Applicable
We know who our top performers are.	
We support the growth of our top performers.	
We treat our employees as "assets" in which we need to invest, rather than as "costs" that can be easily reduced.	
We know the real reasons employees leave our company and we use this information to make improvements wherever possible.	
We invest in the development of our people on a regular basis.	
Our people receive continuous feedback on their performance.	
Employees feel they are compensated fairly for their contribution to our firm.	
We provide opportunities for advancement for those who perform well.	
We regularly ask our employees what we can do to improve our workplace.	
Our executives view employee engagement as a top priority.	
We provide coaches to our top performers.	
We quickly transition nonperformers out of the organization.	
Our customers/clients rave about our employees.	
We are viewed as an exceptional place to work.	
We don't have to go after top talent because they usually approach us.	

Please rate your company according to each of the following statements:	Ratings
	4 = All the time 3 = Most of the time 2 = Sometimes 1 = Rarely 0 = Never N/A = Not Applicable
Employees understand how their work contributes to the bottom line of the company.	
Employees would rate their managers as being great to work for.	
Our managers are trained to select, identify, guide, coach, reward, and retain their people.	
Employees know exactly what is expected of them.	
Employees have the tools and skills to perform their jobs satisfactorily.	
My organization knows how much it costs to replace every employee who leaves the organization.	
I believe this is a great place to work.	

Any area with a score of 2 or lower requires immediate attention!

How to Keep Poor Morale from Seeping into the Rest of the Organization

Poor employee morale is a lot like mold. Once it gets into your office, it spreads into every nook and cranny it can find. In order to rid your organization of the damage, you must extricate the source. Sometimes the source is a person or a group of people, and other times it's a policy gone wrong. In either case, you have to identify the source before you can eliminate it. Once you identify the source(s) that are causing unhappiness, you then must take steps to eliminate the problem. Failure to do so will only prolong the suffering.

In their attempts to quickly rectify the problem, most leaders focus on the symptoms rather than the problem. Doing so may provide temporary relief, but, in the end, the problem always resurfaces and results in further damage.

In many situations, executives have a fairly good idea where the problem resides. Rather than confronting the problem, they delay the situation by operating as if things were business as usual. This is a costly mistake. Here's why. Top performers have choices. They don't have to remain in an environment where leaders refuse to manage. In fact, they are repelled when they are forced to work in chaos simply because of poor management. Instead, they'll take their smarts elsewhere with the hope that their new home will be better run than the one they're leaving. For these people, the risks are low. If they're wrong, there will always be another opportunity waiting for them around the corner.

Problem situations rarely improve without intervention. In fact, most worsen if left unattended. Take action the moment you sense there is a problem. It's best to deal with toxic employees immediately to prevent others in the organization from becoming affected.

Poor employee morale is like a virus that quickly spreads from one person to another. Not to mention the damage that occurs when unhappy employees take their disappointment out on unsuspecting customers. I've had meals delivered to me in a manner that closely resembles a hit-and-run scene out of the latest action thriller. I've also searched high and low for help on the sales floor, only to find employees huddled together dissing the latest policy that's been dumped on them (their words, not mine) by the corporate office.

Unhappy employees can contribute to bankruptcy, even when a product seems imperishable. Hostess Foods, the eighty-five-year-old maker of iconic treats such as Twinkies and Ding Dongs and pantry staples like Wonder Bread, is said to have imploded as a result of a strike by the bakers' union. As reported in the *Wall Street Journal*, a bankruptcy judge gave Hostess permission to force the bakers' union to accept a new five-year labor contract that featured an 8 percent wage cut in the first year, new pension plan restrictions, and a 17 percent increase in health-care costs for employees.

The bakers' union went on strike. "Our members decided they were not going to take any more abuse from a company they have given so much to for so many years," said Frank Hurt, the bakers' union president. As a result, all of Hostess's 18,500 workers lost their jobs and the company crumbled. Other factors contributed to the eventual implosion of the company. But most would agree that the Twinkie took its last breath the day the union refused to be squeezed any further.

Imagine for a moment that, early on, Hostess had created and sustained the type of workplace where workers felt they were treated fairly. The idea of joining a union would have been quickly dismissed by their people. The company may have actually listened when trusted employees suggested they change with the times. Hostess might have been able to overcome many of the issues that eventually caused the company to reach its expiration date much earlier than anyone would have ever predicted.

SAS—A Case Study on Out-of-This-World Magnetism

SAS, a U.S.-based leader in business analytics software and services, is an organization worth studying. Rather than beginning with a long list of employee benefits, Jenn Mann, VP of HR wanted to begin our conversation with the reason SAS does what it does for its people. "Most of the staff that we have here are technical. The majority of our employees have an

(continues)

advanced degree," notes Mann. She goes on to point out the importance of knowing your audience and what motivates them. SAS needs to attract and retain knowledge workers. Mann says:

> We have a clear understanding of our employee population and what motivates them. As a result of this we provide them with the following:
>
> - **An opportunity to do stimulating work.** Our employees love to solve problems, see the relevance of what they do and how it impacts the customer. They get plenty of that at SAS.
> - **Empowering management philosophy.** Creativity and innovation isn't something you can force. You have to provide an environment where people feel inspired and motivated. We allow employees to take risks, which is where innovation comes from.
> - **World-class work environment.** Companies like Google come to campus to see what is possible in terms of work environments.

SAS makes it a point to ensure that people want to come to work every day. Its campus is based on collaboration. All you have to do is peer into one of the cafes to experience what this really means. Of course, you can't have a world-class work environment without the conveniences of home nearby. Most recently, the company added an on-site pharmacy where employees can go to fill prescriptions quickly with small co-pays. On campus you can also find watch repair, car detailing, and (as previously described) even a nail and hair salon. There is something for everyone on campus, including summer camp for your kids, which includes technology classes taught by SAS employees.

When it comes to magnetism at SAS, there are no limits. The icing on the cake is that when you retire, you don't have to leave your rich benefits behind. "Just because you retire, doesn't mean you are no longer part of the family," notes Mann. Families of SAS employees and retirees can log into a special website to keep up with the happenings of the company and to sign up for classes and make appointments with on-campus service providers.

The average tenure at SAS is ten years, which is a lifetime for employers who operate in the world of tech.

Signs That Employee Morale Is Tanking Quickly

Clients often ask me how they could have done a better job of noticing that their magnetism is fading. Here are the signs that I tell them to look out for:

Employee turnover is on the rise. If your employee turnover is fairly low and all of a sudden it's not, then you've got a problem. Failure to take notice can result in you being the last man standing. Why? People don't usually roll out of bed one day and decide today is the day they will quit their job without having given it any thought. Somewhere along the line, something's changed. You may not have noticed, but others have. Be honest with yourself and ask, At what point did people go from being fairly happy to thinking, "I need to get the heck out of here?" Consider that your starting point, and take action to prevent others from following suit.

Sick time is on the rise. I remember dragging myself out of bed to get to work because I loved my job so much. I also remember being very miserable in my job, and picking up the phone and, in my best hoarse voice, telling my manager that I was too sick to come into work that day. There is a direct correlation between employee attendance and morale. Heck, I've been told of a number of situations where the job itself was making the employee sick.

Productivity is declining. It's hard to give a job your everything when everyone around you is miserable and doing as little as possible. This happens frequently in places where inexperienced managers act like slave drivers. They yell and scream and hope that fear will drive commitment and productivity. I've yet to see this tactic work on a long-term basis. Have you? Roy Ng, senior vice president and head of business operations for the Cloud Business Unit at SAP, makes it a point to give his people the time and attention they need to flourish. "You can get the team rowing in the same direction much more quickly when they are happy at work," he says. Ng goes on to point out that this alignment results in higher productivity: "You can run back and forth all day long. If you don't score a point, you lose."

Employees are running on automatic pilot. Employees who used to do an amazing job are now coasting. It's as if they are counting the days to retirement, which is particularly disturbing when most of the staff aren't close to retirement age. Employees become apathetic when they believe no one would notice if they didn't bother to show up today or, in some cases, for the entire month. Think of a time when people were engaged. What, if anything, changed in the work environment that may have caused this shift in employees' behavior?

Customer complaints are increasing. The airline industry is a perfect example of a sector that has experienced huge dips in employee morale and major increases in customer complaints. How many airlines can you name where you recently received great customer service? I can only think of one—Turkish Airlines—but unfortunately it doesn't fly where I usually need to go.

I have several neighbors who work for different airlines, and they are simply miserable at work. Cutbacks in crew, benefits, and communication have caused these companies to take a nosedive in the employee morale department. Customers have flown the coop and have hit the road. My friends dream every day of following suit.

Revenue is decreasing. Your sales team used to be the best in the industry and now they are no longer in the top ten. It's difficult for salespeople to be driven and to sell when they know the organization is unable to deliver on what is promised. A decline in revenue indicates that there may be some rumblings going on under the hood of your organization. Run some diagnostics to determine what needs to be fixed so you can get your revenues humming again.

Quality is down. Has this ever happened to you? You walk into your favorite local business, and you wait in line to place an order. You overhear several employees mumbling about their dissatisfaction with their job or their boss. You wait there patiently until you realize that these employees are more concerned with their conversation than with you. You leave the line, vowing never to return. The quality of service that attracted you to that business has disappeared. There are so many other places customers can spend their money these days that, in their minds, putting up with poor service or quality simply doesn't make sense.

Repeat business is nonexistent. We used to use the same local florist until it became obvious that someone forgot to nurture and maintain the employees. We decided it was time to sever our relationship with this business when the last batch of flowers was dead on arrival. If you are always looking for new business because you have no repeat business, then take a closer look at employee morale. Are your workers happily helping your cause or are they slowly pruning away any chances you may have of repeat business?

Rule of Attraction

U se the Employee Retention Self-Assessment to determine the level of employee engagement in your organization. Provide all your employees with a copy and then compare their answers with those of their managers.

11

Why Employees Really Leave and What You Can Do to Keep Them

When employers ask their people why they are leaving the company, they often hear, "I'm leaving for a better opportunity." That's usually code for, "I hate my boss," "I don't feel valued," "I'm in a dead-end job," or, "You people are too cheap to pay me what I deserve." Then, of course, there is the stock answer, "I'm leaving for more money," which seems to be one of the cleanest ways to break away from an employer. After all, who could argue with that?

When doing the research for this book, I asked many CEOs about the biggest myth regarding the attraction and retention of talent. Almost everyone said that money has little to do with attraction and retention. It's widely understood that people need to make enough money to cover their basic needs, which means that you have to pay a living wage. But if you walk around with an open checkbook, doling out more money the moment you catch wind that an employee is thinking about leaving, you'll eventually learn for yourself that someone else always has deeper pockets. Not to mention, you'll go broke.

I can personally attest to the fact that money alone won't buy you talent, nor will it help you keep talent when other factors are repelling employees. Before I started my consulting practice, I worked as the director of Human Resources for an overnight delivery service. The moment I met the owners of the company, I knew that job had to be mine. It was no secret that the salary being paid was considerably lower than what I could have earned elsewhere—at least 20 percent below market. But that didn't matter to me. I had an opportunity to make my mark and work with some outstanding people.

I got the job and remained in that position for a number of years. Eventually, the pay did become an issue for me, but that was about the time when the owners were in a turf war regarding selling or keeping the business. The winds shifted in the organization, and employees, including me, were no longer treated as individuals. We were treated like disposable assets instead of like treasure. That's when I, along with others, left for "better opportunities."

In order to learn why employees really quit their jobs, I decided to go directly to the source—those who had lied on their way out the door. Here are several of the many responses I received when I asked people why they didn't tell their employers the real reason for their departure.

Stephen C. Murphy, marketing manager
at a small financial services firm

The Situation: I was only twenty-three years old, and I had already climbed as high as I could at the small company I worked for. It got to the point where I stopped learning, and work became a chore instead of a challenge. With no opportunities to learn and a lack of real mentorship, I knew it was time to go.

The Lie: When I finally found a new job and decided it was time to give my two weeks' notice, I used salary as my crutch. I had built close relationships with my coworkers, and I thought it would be a slap in the face to tell them I had "graduated" from working at their company. When they asked if they could counteroffer, I named a number that I knew they could not match, even though it was above the actual new salary I was offered. My boss knew he could not afford this new salary and wished me the best of luck.

I say I lied to protect those around me, but in reality I was probably protecting myself. I did not want to burn a bridge and sacrifice the relationships I had built, so I bent the truth in my exit interview. I don't regret the decision, because we still maintain a strong relationship to this day.

Jim Hathaway, vice president of marketing for an ad agency

The Situation: The president of the company was out of touch with reality, stuck in the past, and not responsive to any moves to change and help position the company for future growth and success. She did not empower her teams, despite the fact that team members were in touch with the market and were aware of the client needs that she did not see.

The Lie: I told my boss I was leaving for a job closer to home, simply because it wasn't worth burning a bridge and trying to get her to recognize shortcomings that she lived with for years without change. She is still chugging along and none the wiser.

Sarah Bruckner, senior associate at PAN Communications

The Situation: My last company was a horrible experience and the women in the office continually threw me under the bus and gave me the worst assignments. I went in to my boss and gave my notice after being given an assignment that was the last straw for me.

The Lie: On the spot, I made up that I was starting grad school at Emerson College. I hadn't even checked to see if they had a public relations/communications school or program. I just lied to get out of the company immediately. In reality, I took a two-month hiatus from work until I landed my dream job (where I am now!).

Five Lines Employees Give When Joyfully Leaving Their Companies

It's understandable that an employee like Stephen Murphy did not want to rub salt into the wounds of his coworkers, so he chose to tell a white lie rather than the truth. But in my experience, this is the exception rather than the rule. Be prepared to dig deeper if an employee gives you one of the following stock lines.

1. **It's not you, it's me.** If your employee ends the relationship with this age-old cliché, then you can bet it *is* you. You'll be able to learn more about what you might have done differently to have prevented this employee from breaking up with you if you don't get defensive. Instead, ask what you might have otherwise done that would have ended with a different result. Be prepared to give examples to get this person talking. Asking questions like, "I often wonder if I had spent more time mentoring you, if that would have made a difference? What's your thought on that?" or, "If I would have given you more autonomy and allowed you to run your own projects, might we

not be having this conversation?" can certainly help you learn what you might have done differently and prevent you from making the same mistake twice.

2. **I'm leaving for a better opportunity.** This may be partially true, but there is usually more to this one than meets the eye. Otherwise, the employee wouldn't have given the other opportunity further consideration. Ask targeted questions to help better understand those areas where you may not be as competitive as you think. Be sure to ask if there was a certain point in time at which this employee would not have considered other opportunities. Follow up by asking what changed for her and why.

3. **I don't have another job.** Most people don't leave jobs without having another one lined up. This means that things were either so bad that the employee couldn't take it anymore, or he doesn't want you to know that he just took a job with your competitor. You can test your theory by asking the employee if he'd be willing to stay until a replacement is found. If he says no before you finish your question, then you can assume there is more to this story than the employee is revealing. You aren't going to be able to get the real reason out of him, but you do want to be sure to keep your eyes and ears open, especially if the employee who is departing has a noncompete agreement with your company.

4. **I'm leaving for more money.** Studies consistently show that the majority of employees don't leave companies for more money, although you wouldn't know this if you added up all the people who give this as their reason for quitting. It's usually something else. We do know that people leave their bosses more than they leave their companies, so that would be a

good place to start. Look for patterns. Are the people who are leaving for more money all working for the same boss? If you gave them a counteroffer and they immediately dismissed your offer, most likely it's not about the money. It's about something else.

5. **I wasn't looking. They called me.** I've done enough direct sourcing to know that if an employee is happy, there is nothing I can do or say to interest her in an interview. Somewhere along the line, discontent has set in, and there is nothing much you can do to save this relationship. Instead, focus your efforts on finding out if the remaining members of your staff are content or if they are ripe to take a call from a third party or another company that knows exactly what to say to pique their interest.

The Fundamental Problem with Exit Interviews

There are a number of problems with exit interviews. The first is that they occur after it's too late to do anything to save the employee, who is now leaving. It's like inviting an inspector into your home after a fire to tell you what you could have done to prevent the damage that has occurred. A little too late, wouldn't you say? You would have been much better served had you taken preventative measures and invited the inspector in beforehand. The same holds true for employee retention. Taking preventative measures along the way will allow you to make course corrections and possibly keep good employees from leaving.

The second problem with exit interviews is the validity of the data gathered. Think about it. Would you advise your daughter to tell her boss that the real reason she is leaving is that she works for a jerk? I think not. Most likely, you'd tell your daughter that it's best not to burn any bridges.

You might also tell her that it's really unlikely much will change even if she decides to be completely honest, so why take the risk?

Magnetic Leader Marla Kaplowitz

CEO Marla Kaplowitz of New York City–based MEC North America, one of the world's top media agencies, is frequently on the front lines gathering intelligence. Kaplowitz believes employee retention is about fulfillment, which means different things for each person. "You have to really understand who the person is, not just the employee," notes Kaplowitz. To do that, you have to take the time to get to know the employee so that you can understand what is happening beyond nine to five.

Kaplowitz cites, as an example, knowing why it's important that an employee be on the 5:00 P.M. train home. He may need to pick his child up from day care. If you know this, you can meet the employee where he is. But you have to spend time with him to understand this.

Kaplowitz is on a mission to get to know the employees at MEC. She has management breakfasts on a monthly basis, and conducts town hall meetings at remote offices. By doing this, she has found that she has become more approachable. People are willing to reveal more of themselves to her, and she is able to meet them where they are. She encourages her management team to get to know the people who work for them.

You might say that Kaplowitz is performing "stay interviews" throughout the day. This approach allows her to have a good handle on the pulse of the organization so she can make course corrections along the way, instead of taking action after a mass exodus.

If you decide to do exit interviews, consider hiring a third party to conduct them. I've had clients engage me to do this, and they are always quite surprised by how honest people are when they are speaking with someone who doesn't work for the company. This type of unfiltered information has allowed my clients to make significant changes, which have included removing the manager who, if given the opportunity to conduct the exit interview, would have edited out the parts that related to his poor leadership.

The third problem with exit interviews is that the people administering these interviews are merely checking off the boxes, especially if they work in organizations that have high turnover. They have no investment in the results, as this is typically done in understaffed Human Resource departments, or in some cases this function may even be outsourced. Try doing a few of these yourself, and you'll quickly see that the information you are gathering usually isn't worth the paper it's written on.

Instead of asking, "Why are you leaving?" you should be asking, "Why did you first start thinking about leaving? What, if anything, could we have done at that time to demonstrate to you that staying would have been a better choice for you?" At least now you have data that you can use to identify those areas where more attention is needed, especially if people keep telling you they became disenchanted at a similar point in time—say, after ninety days on the job, when they realized the job was nothing like it had been described when they were hired.

Stay Interviews

Stay interviews are done while the employee is still in your employ and are preventative in nature. These types of interviews may be part of a climate survey, conducted to measure the temperature in your organization.

Stay interviews are much more effective than exit interviews, especially if you have high levels of trust in your organization. If people feel they can be honest without fearing retribution, they are more likely to speak their minds. You don't have to conduct these interviews one on one, which is a good thing for those employers that have workforces larger than ten people. I've conducted these types of interviews with groups of people, commonly called focus groups.

The clients who have been most successful using this approach are the ones who consistently demonstrate that they are willing and able to make changes based on what is reported. They are also willing to report back on those areas where they are unable or unwilling to address particular issues. This way, employees don't feel their comments have fallen into some black hole.

Following is an example of a significant outcome that resulted from such an initiative.

The Tile People versus the Carpet People

A client of mine who was running a technology company that included a light manufacturing facility was losing key employees. He and his partner sensed there was more to the story than just people leaving for better opportunities. I was hired to conduct focus groups with the members of their team. The groups openly shared with me their concerns, and kept mentioning the tile people and the carpet people. At the time, I was new to the technology industry, and I didn't want to reveal to the employees that I wasn't familiar with their jargon. By the third meeting, I could no longer stop myself from asking what they were referring to when they talked about the tile people and the carpet people. One brave soul told me that the tile people were those employees who stood on tile all day working in the light manufacturing area and the carpet people were those on the other side of the door, who worked in nice offices with plush carpeting.

While debriefing the CEO and president, I mentioned this phenomenon of the tile people and the carpet people and the door that stood between them. The CEO was stunned, as he had no idea there was such a divide in his company. He mentioned that every morning he went into the plant and said hello to the employees. He purposely left the door open so people could come through to the offices freely. Unbeknownst to him, the CFO, whose office was right beside the plant, would close the door when he came in so he could concentrate.

This action had created a feeling of "us versus them," which was creating havoc and unwanted turnover in the organization. This never would have been revealed in an exit interview. Or, if it had been, the information would have likely been discounted as the gripes of a few people, rather than as a central concern of an entire group of workers. The CEO immediately removed the door, thus eliminating the problem.

Immediately following the focus meetings, I shared a compilation of my findings, along with recommendations, with the CEO. Several days later, the CEO released a detailed memo summarizing the outcomes of the focus groups, areas where improvements would be made, and situations (e.g., new work space) where changes would not be made immediately or at any foreseeable time. Later, he reported back to me that the mood throughout the building changed considerably. It's been fifteen years since we worked together on this particular project, and this CEO has moved on to another organization. Whenever we speak, he still recalls the value of the work we did together and the impact this project had for him personally, as well as for the company.

Rule of Attraction

R eplace exit interviews with stay interviews. Stay interviews are routinely conducted while workers are in your employ. The interviews may be part of a climate survey (similar to the Employee Retention Self-Assessment), which measures the temperature in the organization. Smaller organizations may conduct informal stay interviews over breakfast or lunch, with key members of the executive team posing the questions.

The Donut Principle

Historically, when one good employee departs, the rest soon follow. Before long, all that is left is a big fat hole in the middle of the organization where talent once resided. I call this the donut principle. Surrounding the hole is a sprinkling of mediocre workers.

A lot of organizations these days are fat and happy. Their hallways are filled with leaders who continue to drink the Kool-Aid. These people are afraid to tell executives like yourself that the organization is bursting at the seams with an abundance of mediocre workers. Telling the truth might result in being sent out to pasture. So instead, they become part of the problem. They become mediocre leaders.

How to Prevent the Hole from Forming

You can prevent this donut hole from forming by getting out of your office more and paying close attention to what's really going on in your organization. Following are clues to look for.

Signs of Happiness

Happiness at work is, for many people, about the social connection. That's all fine and good, unless people only feel connected with one other person, which is often the case. When that person departs, the remaining employee feels little reason to stay. In fact, it's not uncommon for this employee to follow his only friend to the next organization.

You can prevent this from happening by creating a cohesive workplace where people enjoy the company of one another, a workplace where people are actually encouraged to have fun. Samantha DiGennaro, founder and CEO of DiGennaro Communications, a New York–based PR agency, understands the power of connections at work. Her company subsidizes activities like Bowling Night, an annual scavenger hunt, and Friday happy hours, where different employees mix cocktails to wind down each week. "We work very rigorously in our talent-vetting process to ensure that we hire employees who are not only well qualified, but also fun . . . with diverse backgrounds and extracurricular interests . . . to build a culture of really interesting and fun people," explains DiGennaro. Having fun at work makes good business sense because when employees feel a connection to the rest of the people in their workplace, they will think twice about leaving.

It's not uncommon to see Peter Rinnig, owner of QRST's, at a punk rock concert sitting right next to his employees. His employees cite this as one of the many reasons they enjoy working at QRST's. This type of bonding must be authentic, or your employees will quickly realize that you are there in body only. Especially if you sit through the entire concert with earplugs in your ears!

Tight-Knit Teams

A tightly knit team can withstand the upheaval that often takes place when a member defects. Do your team members tend to sit with one another at lunch? Do they share parts of their lives that are usually reserved for people they consider friends? You can accelerate team bonding by providing team members with an opportunity to get to know one another better, without the distractions of everyday work life. Off-sites greatly accelerate the bonding of work teams.

In a perfect world, you'd be whisking your group off to exciting places like Avignon or Sicily, like Ed Kushins, founder and CEO of HomeExchange, does for his people. Maybe one day this will be possible for you, but for now, a day by the ocean or an afternoon near a lake may be just the ticket to help employees let their guard down, so that others can get to know what's behind all that armor. Community service projects for team members can serve double duty. They are a great way of giving back to the community, and, at the same time, they allow employees an opportunity to view one another in a different light.

Work Spaces That Work

Have you noticed lately that some of your employees have isolated themselves from people they used to sit with? This could be a sign that they are slowly letting go or they feel disconnected. Pay attention to the layout of your work space. Is it conducive to people hanging out and exchanging ideas, or are there walls and doors all around?

The first time I walked into the offices of Monster, I stepped right into the Monster Den, where chairs were strategically placed to encourage employees to hang out with one another. SparkNET has its own version, which CEO Chris Knight refers to as the beanbag Kumbaya center, a place where people can stop and flop.

E-mail marketing software company AWeber is on the move again due to growth. CEO and founder Tom Kulzer is aware of the restrictions physical work space has on cohesiveness and collaboration. If you plan on visiting AWeber's new offices, be sure to look both ways before crossing the room. "All the desks will be on wheels, so employees can more easily collaborate with one another."

A Sense of Family

Do you get the sense that employees feel like they are part of the family? Signs that people feel like they are part of a work family include high attendance at office celebrations that are more personal in nature, such as baby showers and birthdays. When making decisions, people take into consideration the impact those decisions will have on others rather than on just themselves. Are people having healthy disagreements or are they agreeing with everything that's being said because they aren't fully invested?

Although there are bound to be some disagreements, family tends to stick together. If you are able to create a family-like feeling in your organization, you will be able to increase the "stickiness" that keeps the team in place through thick and thin.

Magnetic Leader Faruk Boyaci

At the Sirkeci Group Hotels, headquartered in Istanbul, Turkey, company president Faruk Boyaci has taken special care to create a work environment where both employees and guests are treated like family. Boyaci points out that although Turkey has experienced large financial crises over the years, no employees were let go during these hard times. "Our employees know that we care for them not only in our good days, but also in our bad days," notes Boyaci. Treating employees like family also means treating employees with respect. Boyaci prides himself on the fact that there are few layers of management in his organization, which goes along with his philosophy of hiring the right people and empowering them. "Employees do the right thing without waiting for someone to tell them what they should do." Having stayed at one of his hotels, I can assure you that this is certainly the case.

Retiring in Place

Sometimes business owners, CEOs, and other senior executives believe they have a healthy, productive workforce when in fact the middle of their organization has already fallen out. Only they are too busy to notice. This tends to happen more often in a weak economy. People who have checked out mentally fear what might happen if they leave their organization for another company where they will have no seniority. So instead, they clog up the arteries of organizations like yours, and they remain. They show up every day, only they are never really present. They do what they need to do, yet rarely do more. They no longer share ideas freely because their minds are elsewhere. Their indifference often spreads like a virus throughout the rest of your workforce.

Don't look to your employee turnover numbers to diagnose those who are in this current state, as they have yet to be counted. Rest assured, the moment the economy shifts into full gear, these people will depart. You may be thinking that's great, as they are really not doing much of anything right now. That may be true, but none of us is smart enough to predict when the spigot will be fully turned on and the global economy will be flush with jobs again. Do you still believe you can afford to continue to ignore those who have retired in place?

Why Mediocrity Is on the Rise

Can you think of one great company that got where it is today by being mediocre? I can't. However, I can certainly think of some very successful companies, like Circuit City, Borders, and Saab, that went down in flames quickly when they went from exceptional to mediocre.

The main reason mediocrity is on the rise is that executives are so focused on shareholder value and moving their organizations forward that they don't take the time to look back to see if anyone is even following them. In their drive to increase the value of their organizations, they forget about the people side of the equation.

Mediocrity in Action

I was recently invited to attend a summit where thought leaders were being brought in from around the United States to discuss best practices in leadership. We were asked, as part of the registration process, to sign up in advance for the sessions we would be attending. One session in particular stood out for me. The topic was "Engaging Your Average-Rated Workforce." Why did it catch my attention? Because I could not understand why you would want to invest resources in what appears to be a poor investment. What if, instead, you got rid of those average performers and replaced them with high performers? What if you reinvested your money in those people you know you could take from great to outstanding? I pondered this for a while and then returned to the online registration to make my final choices, only to find that the session on "Engaging Your Average-Rated Workforce" was the only one that was completely full. What does that tell you about the state of most businesses and their workforce?

It doesn't take much to stand out in the crowd these days!

Here's an example of how mediocre performance becomes acceptable, and in some cases the norm, in organizations. The executive team leaves the office for a two-day planning session, where they come up with ideas for new products and services. It's a rare executive who will actually challenge the rest of the team by asking unpopular questions such as, "Do our people have the skills and capacity to handle these new initiatives?" And if the answer is no, to ask, "What as a company are we prepared to do about this?" Of course, doing something means that you would have to address the issue of mediocre performance, which means you might have to make some unpleasant decisions regarding staff. Most likely, you would have to reallocate financial resources, including those earmarked for executive bonuses, and use that money to raise the skill levels of those who have the potential to be better than average. It's no wonder that mediocrity has become the new norm.

What if, instead, executives focused on employee engagement, which includes ridding the organization of mediocrity? After all, how many people are willing to do whatever it takes to help the organization excel when they are working alongside others who could care less about giving it their all. According to the Towers Perrin *Closing the Engagement Gap: Global Workforce Study,* 2007–2008, high-engagement firms grow their earnings per share (EPS) at a faster rate (28%) while low-engagement firms experienced an average EPS growth rate decline of 11.2 percent. This is certainly a topic worth further consideration.

Identifying Your Keepers

You can blame stupid business decisions for declines in revenue and failing companies, but at the end of the day people, not companies, make these decisions. Specific people may have gotten you where you are today, but that doesn't necessarily mean they are the ones who are the "keepers" going forward.

Magnetic Leader Brett Rose

People change, as do organizations. People outgrow their companies, and sometimes their companies outgrow them. Great leaders like UNCS's founder and CEO Brett Rose recognize this and address these issues before they become problems. The Ft. Lauderdale, Florida, company is a wholesale distributor that specializes in supplying retailers with discounted excess inventory and overstock from product manufacturers.

(continues)

Rose's company has achieved high levels of success over the past ten years. To get to the next level, Rose understands that he may have to make some unpopular decisions. In the past, whenever possible he has promoted from within. He doesn't know if he will be able to continue to do so as his company goes through the next cycle of growth. But he is not letting that stop him from trying. Rose is beginning to think of what he needs to do today to prepare his people to scale with the company. He continues to hire for potential and moves people into roles where they can maximize their contributions. He's also prepared to hire from the outside if that's what's required to move the company to the next level.

Here's a list of questions that I provide to my clients to help them determine whether an employee is a keeper. I recommend you ask yourself these questions as well.

1. If this person applied for a job with you today, would you hire her?
2. Does this person still have potential?
3. Does this person still model the behaviors that you, as a company, value?
4. What would be the impact on the organization if this employee left the company tomorrow?
5. Is he still willing to do whatever it takes to get the job done?
6. Is this employee continually looking to improve herself?
7. Do her strengths far outweigh her weaknesses?
8. Are this employee's background and skills still appropriate, given the direction you are now taking your business?
9. Is he still happy coming to work every day?

10. Is it in this employee's best interest to remain with your organization?

What to Do with the Rest

Sometimes it's possible to bring people back into the fold, especially if they haven't strayed too far. You do this by addressing specific issues that are keeping them from fully contributing to the organization. It's certainly worth a try, especially if these employees have a solid performance record, show potential, and demonstrate a willingness to improve.

Other times, it's in everyone's best interest to sever ties, as it's doubtful things will get better. In fact, in most cases, matters will only get worse. We'll discuss how you can do this with the least amount of disruption in Chapter 15.

How to Prevent People from Slipping through the Cracks

Executives and managers are fixated on results when in fact they should be focusing their efforts on creating a workplace where employees are comfortable discussing how they really feel about work. A workplace filled with happy, productive employees will deliver the results you need.

It takes work and commitment to keep a good employee from slipping away. But you have to be willing to put the time in to make this so. You have to be fully present so that you are aware of changes that are going on around you. For example, if a good employee is going through a difficult time personally, which is impacting her work, you have a decision to make. You can provide additional support and flexibility to the employee or you can suggest the employee take a leave or resign until such time as she can fully commit to her job. Doing nothing and pretending that things will get back to normal without an intervention will do more damage than good. Sometimes you have to let go of someone in order for them to come back to you. Other times you can help the employee get back on track if you take note and action before the employee slips too far away to reach your hand.

Rule of Attraction

Pay attention to the signs that indicate a donut hole may be forming in your organization. Frequently ask yourself the following questions:

Do people appear to be happy at work?

Are team members working well with one another?

Are employees working side by side or in isolation?

Do people seem to feel they are part of the work family?

A "no" to any of these questions indicates that good people may seep out of your organization. Plug the hole while there's still time.

Rules of Engagement

Magnetic retention is all about connecting with the hearts and minds of your employees so that you have the stickiness that will keep people happily in your employ. One company that does this particularly well is Apple. I've been an Apple user for more than five years now, and I visit my local Apple Store frequently. I know I shouldn't be surprised, but I'm still amazed that the cast of employees who waits on me rarely changes. Apple employees are evangelists. They are on a mission to spread the word about Apple products because they truly believe in their hearts and their minds that your world will be better because of the work they do. The company has done a great job of creating a highly engaged workforce. You can do the same.

How to Create an Environment of Highly Engaged Workers

Creating a work environment that results in high levels of employee engagement takes work and constant attention. However, the results speak for themselves. The business owners, CEOs, and other senior executives who have created this type of environment reap more than financial rewards. They go home every night knowing that they've improved the lives of those who work for them. They have less stress, knowing that their people will do the right thing whether they are standing next to them or are working halfway around the globe. Having a highly engaged workforce frees these CEOs and senior executives to focus on innovation and business growth. Following are some of the ways they accomplish this.

Work Environment

In spite of what you'd like to believe, the physical work environment matters to many. I remember working in one of Boston's premier buildings, which had views you could die for, if you actually had a window in your office. I was stuffed inside what could have been a closet, along with another employee. The high-paid consultants, who were out of the office most of the day, were given the offices with a view while the support staff were in offices like mine. This was one of those workplaces where you rarely saw anyone smile. Workers would stampede out the door the moment lunchtime arrived. At the time, I thought they did this in order to get their daily dose of Vitamin D, but, in retrospect, there was much more to this situation. Being treated like second-class citizens did little to create an engaged workforce.

"I wouldn't ask people to sit in places where I wouldn't want to sit," states Tom Kulzer, founder and CEO of AWeber Communications. "I keep this in mind as I'm building our new facility." Kulzer's motto is, "Treat your customers and your employees the way you'd want to be treated." He and his executive team live by these words. "Everyone around here does whatever needs to be done, regardless of rank. Even if that means cleaning the bathroom floor after a flood." He wasn't kidding. After my interview with Kulzer, he sent me a picture of his COO mopping the bathroom floor. I'm sure if this had happened at my old company, one of us underlings would have been handed a mop and sent into the bowels of the organization to clean up the mess. Come to think of it, that person probably would have been me!

The Nature of the Work

Employees who are most engaged are those who feel they have a clear influence on the way work gets done. It is important to most people to have challenging, creative, and varied work that allows them to utilize their old skills and develop new ones. At all levels of the organization, it's important that employees feel that the work they do has a clear purpose and meaning.

The key here is to recognize that this holds true at *all* levels of the organization. I've supervised mail clerks who took great pride in their work, knowing that if they failed to do their jobs well, others in the organization would be unable to perform their work. These employees had a clear purpose and understood the importance of their contribution to the overall success of the company.

Sometimes you have to help people connect the dots, as many will not realize how their work impacts the rest of the workforce or the customer. A good practice is to occasionally take workers from different levels of the organization on customer visits. This allows them to experience firsthand why their work really does matter.

Belief in the Mission and the Vision of the Organization

I once worked for a financial consulting firm where we made wealthy nonprofits even wealthier. I have to say, that was a mission that I had a hard time wrapping my head around, and it showed every day. To say that I was disengaged would be putting it mildly.

Sometimes people don't believe in the mission and the vision of the organization because they have no idea what it is. Perhaps that's because this changed somewhere along the way and management forgot to inform the rest of the organization. Possibly, it was never fully explained when the employee was brought on board.

SparkNET has the company's core values displayed front and center for all to see. Chris Knight had a Core Values Mural wall designed for the first floor of his new building, which employees and visitors see immediately upon entering the building. This type of reminder is much more effective than sending out an annual memo to all your employees repeating the company's mission and values or stuffing this information into the employee handbook, where it remains hidden until the employee tears out the page to use as fireplace kindling.

If you happen to have an employee in your workplace who doesn't feel any connection to the mission and the goals of the organization, do yourself and the employee a favor. Release this employee, so he is free to find a workplace where he feels a connection and can thrive.

A Workplace Where People Feel Valued

I've done my best work when working for an organization where I felt valued, and I did my worst work (at the financial consulting firm) when I didn't feel valued. Employees operate best when they feel like they matter.

As a business owner, CEO, or senior business leader, you may be sending the message that employees matter. However, busy middle managers may not be doing the same. By the time employees in the middle or the bottom of the organization receive the message (if they do at all), it sounds nothing like the one you intended. That's why it's important that you communicate directly with employees whenever possible. "I always pass along e-mails that I receive from customers thanking us for a job well done. I make it a point to print out the e-mail and hand deliver it to the employee who delivered the job, so they know they did a good job and that our customer knows this as well," states Rinnig.

Marla Kaplowitz makes it a point to understand that her people have a life outside work, so she doesn't take note when an employee dashes out the door to make the 5:00 P.M. train. This is one of the many ways that Kaplowitz shows her employees they are highly valued. She doesn't make them choose between having a career and having a family. She encourages them to have one whole happy life.

Attention to Employee Input

Gallup's research on employee engagement found that those who were highly engaged felt that their opinions matter at work. As already mentioned, Kaplowitz uses town hall meetings and monthly management breakfasts to gather opinions from employees: "This builds a stronger connection and helps people understand that their opinions matter," she notes. You can do the same, even if your workforce is global. Skype and Google+ are both great tools to help you stay better connected with people who may not work at the same location as you.

Employee Empowerment

It should come as no surprise that there is a direct correlation between employee empowerment and employee engagement. I talked at length with Niki Leondakis about this. "We look for people who we believe genuinely enjoy making others happy. We inspire our people to take care of our guests in their own way. We don't have a trillion standard operating procedures regarding great service." That's because Leondakis has built a culture of trust. She empowers her people to make decisions, and, in return, they take great care of Kimpton guests. Kimpton Hotel employees are indeed a highly engaged workforce.

Compare this with the approach at most organizations, where employees have to go up a layer or two in order to do right by the customer. I'm going through this experience with Sears. I've had three visits from a Sears repair person to fix a dehumidifier that is under warranty; the wrong parts have been delivered twice and the manager of customer service refuses to speak directly with me. When I spoke with the customer service representative, she mentioned that Sears had sent out new machines to customers who kept receiving the wrong parts. However, she didn't have the power to authorize a replacement without the approval of the manager, who refuses to speak with customers. Did I mention that this appliance retails for less than $200? I know how frustrated I am. I can't imagine how frustrating it must be for the employees of Sears who aren't trusted to do the job they've been hired to do. Not to mention how much money Sears has wasted, and the company still doesn't have a satisfied customer. I can assure you that things would be quite different if Leondakis were president of Sears!

Supplying the Necessary Tools

It's difficult to be fully committed to doing whatever it takes at work when your company refuses to provide you with the tools you need to get the job done. I've known people who started bringing in tools from home because the company refused to invest in what they needed to do their jobs well. After a while, these people tired of carrying what appeared to be a tool shed back and forth to the office. They stayed home one day with their shed and never returned to work.

If you want your people to perform at optimal levels, then provide them with the resources they need to get the job done. Anything less is a disservice to the employee and to your customers.

Support for Employees

Executives talk a good game around the subject of innovation, yet few put their money where their mouth is. Instead, heads roll when great ideas turn out to be not-so-great business decisions. In organizations like these, you'd be crazy to stick your neck out without a body to support you. So most don't.

Eve Bayer of Winkle, a market research agency headquartered in Amsterdam, is fortunate to experience what it's like to feel supported, which is a good thing because she's located in New York City while her boss is in Amsterdam. "Winkle is not like every other company," notes Bayer. "The culture of the company is to have each other's back, which is not typically the case in advertising." Bayer is busy building Winkle's first U.S. office and will be working hard to create the same kind of culture that is firmly established at the home office. Demonstrating the kind of support that she is receiving to her own people is high on her list in terms of engagement.

Think about what you can do to make your employees feel more supported. Perhaps you can thank the person who took a risk and tried something unconventional, even though the idea didn't work. Or you can say yes when an employee comes to you requesting time off to deal with personal matters, even though he may not have made a large enough deposit in his time-off bank.

Opportunities to Learn and Grow

Employees who receive company support for growth and development are much more engaged than those who don't.

I was fortunate to work for a company that believed this as well. My employer paid for my MBA, and, in return, I gave the company my heart and soul while I was in its employ. This was a fair deal for all involved. This same company granted me a mentor to help me grow into the position of director of HR, and for that I will always be grateful.

Today, companies are less thoughtful about how they invest in their people. Instead of looking at individual needs, entire departments are required to attend training programs that are, quite frankly, little more than a nice time together. What if, instead, you took some of these dollars and allocated them to your best performers so they could get even better? Or what if you gave these people an opportunity to work one on one with a coach who could help them build on their strengths? This is how you build a rock-solid team *and* an engaged workforce that will stick around longer than most.

Low-Cost Ways to Show Employees They're Valued

Businesses of all sizes can compete for talent without breaking the bank. Yes, you still need to pay competitive wages to get people in the door, but it's the perks that will help increase your magnetism and your retention. When it comes down to it, it's better to work for a company that cares about you than a company that doesn't. And from a company standpoint, that makes it better to care than to not care.

Here are a number of low-cost ideas for businesses that want to show employees they are highly valued. Go ahead, place a check mark next to all the ones you are willing to try.

Discretionary Time: The New Definition of Employee Wealth

I had a number of friends, back in the nineties, who were employed at big companies like Fidelity and the now defunct

Digital. They all made a heck of a lot of money in comparison with their counterparts elsewhere. However, they sacrificed much in return for their above-average salaries. They gave up their lives, as they were working around the clock and on weekends. They continued to do so until they either burned out, quit, or were laid off due a downturn in the economy. These people raised children who then experienced what it was like to see a parent laid off after giving a company everything. Just like the generation before them, these children swore they'd do things differently.

These children are now your employees, and many of their parents are still in the workforce. They've learned many lessons along the way, the most important being that time is precious and cannot be replaced. Today's workers, both young and old, place a high value on discretionary time, as that is the new definition of employee wealth. That's good news for businesses of all sizes, as time is the one thing you can all afford to give. Here are five ways to increase the "wealth" of your people.

1. **Flex time.** Some organizations require employees to be at work during core hours, and then allow employees to set their schedule around this. Others allow employees to put in hours at their own discretion. This shouldn't be a problem if you measure people on results instead of face time, which is something I highly recommend. Most companies require employees to have a set schedule so managers can plan for coverage. The schedule may be adjusted to accommodate personal situations like doctor's appointments.

2. **Summer hours.** Employees may work extended hours during other months of the year in exchange for kicking back early on Fridays during the summer months. This allows them to beat the heat as well

as the traffic if they're heading out to the beach for a weekend.

3. **Unlimited vacation time.** Some companies offer their employees what is perceived to be the ultimate benefit: unlimited paid vacation. By showing that they trust their workers, these employers are cultivating a culture of deeper trust. Though the practice is still fairly new, companies report that there is little abuse of the system so far. This benefit is most common at smaller companies, where schedules are easier to coordinate. The idea is certainly gaining popularity as employers recognize that unlimited vacation time is a low-cost way to win loyalty from employees and can help compensate for things like low salaries. This perk also demonstrates to employees that a company values employees' well-being. Warning: don't even consider this benefit unless you have a high-trust culture.

4. **Paid sabbaticals.** I left my job after six years to travel around the world. Perhaps I would still be employed there if my employer had offered paid sabbaticals. Offer month-long sabbaticals after five years of service or two months after ten years of service. This is a great way to separate your company from the pack, as paid sabbaticals are rare outside academia. And while you are at it, don't forget to post this benefit front and center on your website for all to see.

5. **Parental leave.** Although it's not particularly generous compared with other nations, parental leave in the United States is granted to most new moms under a federal mandate. Some states take this further and guarantee paid leave. That's great for the moms, but what about the dads? More than fifty

nations, including most Western countries, guarantee paid leave for new fathers. But in the U.S. (among other countries), there is no such thing as mandated paid leave for new fathers. But that doesn't mean you can't be the first on your block to offer this to your employees. You can immediately differentiate your company by making sure all employees are eligible for paid time off after the birth or adoption of a child.

Nurturing the Hearts, Souls, and Stomachs of Employees

Those employers who connect with the hearts, souls, and stomachs of their employees stand a much greater chance of retaining their workers than those who don't. We've all heard stories of the wonderful benefits Google provides for their employees. I know most of you don't have a Google-sized budget, but that shouldn't prevent you from making similar connections. Here are six ways you can do this:

1. **Employee interest groups.** Opower is a small company with huge benefits, and it really understands the advantages of employee interest groups. Opower seems to have something for everyone, including a foodie interest group called Ofoodies and a soccer interest group known as Osoccer. On a recent visit to the company, President Obama stated, "This looks like a fun place to work!" Other interest groups that can be easily created include book clubs, biking clubs, and theater groups. The sky is the limit when it comes to assembling these clubs. Follow your employees' interests, and they will lead you to the right group(s) for your company.

2. **Fully stocked kitchens.** I don't know about you, but I have a hard time concentrating on an empty stomach. Of course, most employees are free to leave

the building to pick up a snack, but that usually winds up turning an intended ten-minute break into a half-hour excursion. Many of my clients, including QRST's, keep the kitchen well stocked in order to fuel the minds and bodies of their employees. Companies that are more health conscious include fresh fruit as well as healthy snacks. Employers like Opower take this one step further by having fresh organic milk delivered to its offices daily from a local provider.

3. **Not your average free lunch.** There's the Friday lunchtime pizza delivery, and then there is lunch made daily by the boss's mom, which is what happens at UNCS. You don't have to hire your own personal sushi chef to provide your fish-loving employees with a healthy lunch. Instead, you can arrange for trays of sushi to be delivered to the office once a month or, if your budget permits, more frequently. If you have your own cafeteria, like AWeber or SparkNET, you can provide your employees with healthy meals that will have them coming back for seconds.

4. **Community service.** I thought I knew what there was to know about community service until I met Harris Rosen, founder and CEO of Rosen Hotels & Resorts, based in Orlando, Florida. At a cocktail gathering, Rosen joked with me, saying that his kids thought he was giving too much darn money away. Rosen puts his money where his mouth is. For more than a decade, Rosen has taken an ambitious and transformational approach to helping Haiti, where as many as a third of his hotel employees have roots. "That little country has just suffered so," he says. Community service runs through the veins of the organization, as Rosen encourages his employees to

get involved by helping choose the causes to support, and he provides employees with plenty of time and opportunities to volunteer. Giving people the time to impact the lives of others is something that money cannot buy.

5. **Going green.** Preferred parking and/or subsidies for those who purchase and drive hybrid vehicles is just one of the many ways that employers can support a cause—going green—which is close to the hearts of many, especially younger employees. Providing employee incentives for those who bike to work, offering subsidies for bus or train passes, or even contributing a monthly allowance toward car shares, such as Zipcar, can go a long way toward nurturing the souls of those who strongly believe in minimizing their carbon footprint.

6. **Employee wellness for all.** One of my clients reimburses employees for purchases related to fitness (up to $300 per year). Typical items reimbursed include gym memberships, running shoes, yoga mats, bicycles, and so on. Another brings fitness instructors on site so that employees can stay in shape at their workplace. Rosen takes this one step further. His company recently debuted a new employee medical center that includes rooms for services such as digital mammography, bone mineral density scans, and nutritional counseling. By doing so, Rosen feels that he is providing his employees with better-quality care. Employees are more apt to seek care when symptoms first arise rather than to put off treatment, as they are able to visit the clinic while on the clock. In a recent article, Rosen was quoted as saying that he calculates that, over the two-decade run of the program, he has unexpectedly saved $215 million.

And this number does not include how much he may have saved by reducing employee turnover.

Something for Everyone

Employees come in all shapes and sizes and have different wants and needs. Here are some ideas for low-cost perks that are bound to connect with a host of employees.

1. **Canine colleagues.** Got an office full of dog lovers? Then invite house-trained visitors to join the team. A number of organizations, including Opower, have rolled out the welcome mat for well-behaved dogs. One would think a china shop would discourage or even prohibit pets from going near their delicate wares. But that's not the case at Replacements, the world's largest china retailer. The company allows its employees to bring well-behaved pets to work every day. According to public relations manager Lisa Conklin, these animals are less destructive than their owners. "We break things all the time," says Conklin. "But I've never seen a pet break our china."

2. **Work–life balance—really!** Everybody talks about it, but few are actually able to deliver. What if you were able to create an atmosphere where it is okay to leave the office before 8:00 P.M.? You can, if you have a high-trust workforce and you measure people on results rather than face time. Imagine what it would be like to work in a place like this. You'd have to be crazy to quit!

3. **Dress codes that fit today's workforce.** The problem with most dress codes today is that they don't really fit. The one-size-fits-all model doesn't work. Yet, employers insist on squeezing staff members into

these policies and then getting upset when employees burst out of the seams. Naturally, it's important for those interacting with clients to be dressed appropriately. But that doesn't mean the rest of the organization needs to come in dressed to meet the queen.

In a recent interview in *Entrepreneur* magazine, Sir Richard Branson, English business magnate and founder and chairman of the Virgin Group, discusses his distaste for ties. "Virgin just got into the banking business with the acquisition of Northern Rock, a British bank that we are gradually rebranding Virgin Money. In British banking, few things strike terror in the heart of a customer quite as much as the prospect of facing a tie-wearing, three-piece-suited bank manager across a huge mahogany desk. So we redesigned the banks and we got rid of the ties," says Branson. He goes on to say, "I have always hated ties, maybe because I've never seen the point. They are uncomfortable and serve no useful purpose. I am lucky to have always worked for myself, and therefore have never been a victim of corporate dress codes." Let's face it. Branson runs a fine operation, even for a man who doesn't believe in dressing like everyone else. Perhaps there is something to be said for this cutting ties with ties thing and allowing people to feel comfortable at work.

4. **Tech neutrality.** I could never work for my brother because at his company, PCs rule. I'm more of a Mac kind of gal, as I find them easier to use. I can't imagine what it must be like to go to work every day and be forced to use a particular type of computer because that's what's required. I understand that, years ago, Macs and PCs didn't play nicely together, but much has changed since Al Gore invented the

Internet. Some companies, like Cisco and Opower, allow their employees to choose the type of computer they are most comfortable working with. Now, that's what I call a revolution. If only I could convince my brother to do the same!

5. **Perks for part-time employees.** Many organizations treat part-time workers like temps. If you provide part-time workers with perks, they'll be acting like full-time workers in no time. In this day and age of companies operating 24–7, it no longer seems equitable to provide benefits only to full-time employees, especially when often it's the part-time workers who are most valuable to the organization. You don't have to offer every benefit to this group of employees, but you can certainly provide them with more than most are currently entitled to.

6. **Laundry service.** Raise your hand if you love doing laundry. Hmmm . . . just as I expected. Few, if any, hands are going up. Employ a service to pick up employees' clothes and drop them back at work, clean and folded. If you are the type of leader who doesn't like hugs, then get out of the way. This is one perk that few have, yet everyone can enjoy.

7. **Housekeepers for all!** In a recent interview with Phil Libin, CEO of Redwood, California–based Evernote, the company that's helping the world remember everything, Libin was asked what people love most about the culture at Evernote. "Probably the thing that we do that people love the most is housekeeping. If you work at Evernote, you get professional housecleaning twice a month." When asked why the company implemented this benefit, he goes on to say, "We thought that we needed to get spouses and significant others on our side. I want the pressure

from them to be, 'You better not be thinking about leaving Evernote.' I don't want the pressure to be, 'Maybe you should think about going somewhere else?'" I think Libin is onto something here. I swear if my husband's company had such a benefit, he'd still be working there today!

8. **Tuition forgiveness.** Young people today are drowning in debt from college loans. Consider throwing them a lifesaver by offering to pay a percentage of tuition owed per year of employment. Or think about offering tuition reimbursement for those who are interested in furthering their education. Your employees get smarter and they bring new ideas back to your company. That's one benefit that gets an "A" from both job seekers and employees.

Rule of Attraction

Make a list of what matters most to the people who work for you. Don't know? Simply ask. Then start implementing programs and practices to strengthen the connection with the minds, hearts, and souls of those who matter.

CHAPTER

14

Why Low Employee Turnover *Isn't* Such a Great Thing

I recently met with a hospital CEO who proudly told me that he didn't need my services because his turnover was less than 3 percent. I sat and listened as he described the situation in more detail to me. When he stopped to take a drink of water, I asked, "What if I were to show you that having such low turnover was as dangerous as having low blood pressure? Would you still say your organization was in fine shape?" He took another sip and quietly said, "Tell me more."

I had a similar discussion with an HR executive from one of the big four accounting firms regarding the dangers of extremely low turnover. Several years ago, the firm did its staffing as usual, assuming that those who weren't on the partnership track would leave voluntarily. What the firm, like many of you, wasn't prepared for was the worst recession since the Great Depression. Accountants hung onto their jobs like oak leaves in winter, clinging far beyond the appropriate season. The firm is now going through a massive spring cleanup, which includes the removal of dead leaves—and it's a chaotic and uncomfortable process for all.

Most successful businesses frequently benchmark other companies in their industry to understand how they are doing in comparison to competitors and best-in-class businesses. They are able to improve their own performance by tailoring and incorporating best practices into their own organizations. I recommend that you compare your employee turnover rates with those of organizations you view as best in class. This will allow you to make slight adjustments along the way, rather than having to take drastic measures down the line.

Too Much Magnetism Isn't a Good Thing

People You'd Rather Release Are Stuck on You

Sometimes you know deep in your heart that someone has outstayed her welcome. Perhaps this individual has peaked, but you truly believe she would once again flourish if she could just get herself unstuck from your organization. Or maybe someone has lost his passion for the job and is preventing the company from moving forward with force. As a business owner, CEO, or other senior executive, you have a job to do. In this case, it's to help this person untether himself from the organization. We'll talk about how to do this in Chapter 15.

The Ones You Don't Want to Keep Will Stick Around

If you've ever witnessed a voluntary layoff then you know exactly what I mean when I say that the employees you'd prefer to divest yourself of are those most likely to hang on. A company decides it's necessary to reduce costs, and it begins with what's easiest to see—employee head count. The company asks for volunteers to leave the company. Those employees the firm hopes will raise their hands choose to stick around while the good people dash out the door with exit packages in hand. Situations like this aren't accidents. In my experience, they happen for two reasons.

The first reason is that you have conflict-averse managers who avoid doing what makes them most uncomfortable, which includes having difficult but necessary conversations about performance and then following through by terminating those who are unable to rise to the occasion. (You may need to look at your own contribution as well, if these managers work for you.) Instead, these types of managers wait until things get really bad, and then they sweep underperforming workers into a pile the moment the company announces the need to cut head count. This approach is extremely harmful to the organization, as it takes months or even years for the "survivors" to get over the trauma that has been unnecessarily thrust upon them. These survivors often witness chopping of headcount with no compassion. Tales of long-term employees being shown the door add to the anxiety. All the while, most are thinking, "When will they be coming for me? Surely I must be next."

My best clients don't do this. Instead, we work together to teach managers how to increase their staff's performance by confronting without conflict. If certain employees are still unable to turn their performance around, we work together to support the manager as he transitions these people out of the firm. Those managers who are unable to apply these new skills often realize that perhaps management isn't where they are best suited. They either leave on their own or they are removed before more damage is done.

The second reason employees you wish would go stick around is that—as we touched upon in Chapter 2—companies often make the fatal mistake of believing that when employees say they are happy to have a job, it means they are happy *in* their jobs. In an economy where jobs are scarce, those people who aren't particularly happy often stay out of fear that they'll never work in this town again.

If, as a business owner, CEO, or other senior executive, you are aware of this, you can take steps to help reengage these workers or to release those you know will never return from the land of disengagement.

The Ones That You Want to Keep Won't Stick Around

Top players want to play with other top players. Never was this phenomenon more evident then when basketball legend LeBron James left the Cleveland Cavaliers to join basketball greats Dwyane Wade and Chris Bosh with the Miami Heat, forming the best threesome the NBA has seen in decades. Reportedly, James said he felt like he let a lot of people down, but the chance to pair up with Bosh and Wade made the decision for him. He said it was what was best for him. The same holds true in business. It's no coincidence that some organizations have a slew of talented people, while others have barely any. It's not uncommon for talented people to move in packs. But you already know this if your pack has left the fold.

You'll End Up Working with Subpar People

When is the last time you heard a CEO say that she was looking to create an unexceptional company? Yet this is what happens when your company hangs on to mediocre and subpar people. You eventually set a new low standard for your organization. This situation is entirely avoidable, particularly in an economy where there are plenty of good workers looking for jobs. You could have raised the bar by replacing subpar people with exceptional employees the moment you noticed something was amiss. Hopefully, it's not too late to take action.

There's No Place for Strong Performers to Advance

Most top performers are high achievers. This means they expect to keep advancing in the organization. Now, think about what happens when there is a huge clog in the system. By that, I mean that people who should have been gone a long time ago show up for work every day (at least physically) and occupy jobs that the high achievers are hoping to obtain. Most would understand if the people in those jobs were exceptional, but all too often this isn't the case. I recently conducted a webinar for BLR on how to be a great boss. I opened by asking participants to signal whether they'd ever worked for a great boss. Sadly, only one person indicated he had. How long do you think these high achievers will stick around? My guess is, not that long.

Mediocrity Can Become the Rule, Rather Than the Exception

Earlier in this book, I talked about how mediocrity was becoming the new norm. Here's how too much magnetism can contribute to this. Let's assume for a moment that you are hiring fairly smart, hard-working people. Review time comes around, and these outstanding people receive the same percentage increase as the people who are rated aver-age. I know you'd like to believe that compensation is a private matter between the boss and the employee, however this is rarely the case. It's not uncommon for employees to know what others make, and this is particularly true around review time. It doesn't take long for people to realize that it's okay to be mediocre. In fact, it's rewarded. Before long, mediocrity becomes the norm rather than the exception.

Compensate those who are contributing the most and don't worry about the impact this will have on those who are mediocre at best.

Opportunity for Growth Is Stunted

I've seen a lot of companies put the brakes on development opportunities because they believe an experienced workforce doesn't need additional training. Resources are allocated elsewhere, and before long innovation and productivity are no more. The company's growth is stunted. Eventually, the good people bail. Good people are always looking to improve, and Humana is a fine example of an organization that continually provides opportunities for its people to soar. "The company does a good job of identifying and developing future leaders," notes Humana executive Paul Kraemer.

You can do the same for your organization, even if it's on a smaller scale. Bring in thought leaders to facilitate a conversation over lunch. Encourage employees to attend seminars that will ensure they continue to grow. Ask a trusted resource to recommend a coach who can come in and provide group coaching for your high potentials. If people aren't asking you to support their development, then perhaps your good people bailed a long time ago and you simply haven't noticed. Consider this your wake-up call.

Why Some Employee Turnover Is Actually Good for Your Organization

In the past several weeks I've had conversations with CEOs who have, in key positions, people who have been with the company thirty-plus years. The departments these employees oversee are basically operating in the Dark Ages.

Functions that in other companies were streamlined and automated a decade ago are still being done manually. No one likes to remove a long-term employee, especially when the person is close to retirement, and I'm certainly not recommending you do so. However, allowing the situation to continue without an intervention can be deeply damaging to the company. In a situation where your employee is nearing retirement, consider working together to come up with a solution that will serve everyone well. For example, if you are able to agree on an exact retirement date, you can then work together to hire and train a replacement. You might also provide this employee with a separation package that will keep him whole until he is able to take advantage of government retirement benefits that he may need to keep him going.

Six Reasons Every Organization Needs *Some* Employee Turnover

1. New Blood Brings New Ideas

If you work in a large organization, then I'm guessing certain things have been done the same way since the day you arrived. Admit it. Even you may not know why some things are done a certain way, but you've accepted it because that's the way things have always been done. Then along comes a new hire who looks at everything with a fresh eye. This employee begins asking questions like, "What's the reason for doing this? Here's what we did at my last company. Do you think it would work here?" Suddenly you realize that somewhere along the line you became one of *those* people. The kind who keeps doing things the same way because that's how it's always been done and no one has ever suggested differently.

A Mouthwatering Story of Innovation

These days, if you are not innovating, you are falling behind. Even nonprofits know this. My family and I are big fans of mobile restaurants, commonly referred to as food trucks. So much so that my son has decided to do his eighth-grade research project on the evolution of this phenomenon that is rolling across America. During his research he found that the University of Massachusetts at Amherst has one truck out the door and another one on the way. These trucks are revenue generators for the university, as they pull in $4,000 to $5,000 per day. They also provide the university with an opportunity to connect with students, as the program was built from scratch with input from students and staff, and is completely self-operated. Students regularly submit ideas and vote for favorite menu iterations on Facebook, and even the truck's name is a product of student input. Food is serious business for the dining services people at UMass, and they work very hard to be sure the dining program enhances campus life for their students. This requires continually innovating to stay competitive with other schools.

So what has your company done recently in terms of innovation? If the answer is nothing, it's time to take your training wheels off and get rolling.

2. New Energy Stimulates Others to Take It Up a Notch.

Have you noticed how the energy level goes up when a new person is thrown into the mix? This occurs when someone new walks into a party as well as when a new employee enters the office. I remember attending a Bat Mitzvah where the family hired a "motivator" to stir things up on the dance floor. This person's sole job was to get people off their chairs and onto the dance floor. The energy in the room shifted dramatically as one by one people joined in.

If you are hiring curious people, they will welcome the new energy. In fact, most will thrive because of it. Perhaps that's because the new person doesn't quite know his limits in the organization, so the sky is the only boundary he knows. Once people see this person is gaining traction, they will join in, even if it's one by one.

Most businesses need to have people leave before they can afford to bring in new staff. If it's been a long time since anyone new has come along, and everyone is sitting quietly in their seats, then it may be time to turn up the volume and get people moving again.

3. New Experiences Lead to Rapid Growth

Inviting new people into the organization is like injecting a breath of fresh air. The experience they bring as a result of their education and work experience cannot be replicated. I remember my first year of employment at the overnight delivery company. I came in, and in one year's time, I got more done than my colleagues had after years in the organization. I had no idea what a difference I had made until I received the company's "Difference Maker of the Year" award, which was a complete surprise. Quite frankly, I had no idea there was even such an award to be had!

Change for many organizations can be hard. But what I've learned over the years is that if you aren't moving forward, you are standing still. There isn't a business I can think of today that, if it kept the status quo, would be in business ten years from now. Change is healthy. Embrace it and teach your people how to deal effectively with the unknown.

4. Diversity Leads to New Business Opportunities

When I first started my career, just about everyone in the workforce looked the same. At least they did to me. Thankfully, a lot has changed since those days. Today, it's not uncommon to walk into the kitchen of any business and feel like you are in the middle of a food court. The blend of nationalities in many organizations reflects the global nature of business in the twenty-first century and the shifting demographics of many countries. Companies that do not have a diverse workforce are missing out on a wealth of opportunities.

Selling in a global economy requires an understanding of the people you are trying to reach. Who better to help you understand these consumers than your own employees—that is, if you have a diverse workforce. People bring different life experiences to the workplace, creating a multiplicity of cultures that makes the organization that much richer.

It's no accident that in some organizations everyone looks the same, comes from the same background, and may even think in the same way. This is often owing to what I have previously referred to as the "halo effect." The scenario goes something like this: the hirer thinks, "He looks like me so he must be a good candidate for this job," or, "We went to the same private university, so this person automatically is in since we know that *everyone* who attended this university (*all* 45,000 of us) is exceptional." It's hard to diversify organizations like these, as few really want to be the first person to crack the barrier. But it's not impossible. Of course, you have to have job openings in order to begin.

5. Challenges to the Status Quo Improve the Business

IBM employed me in the late seventies, so I have firsthand experience working in an environment where employees never challenged the status quo. Things may be quite different there today, but at that time, you simply did what you were told. And, of course, you wore a dark navy suit, even if you were a woman. Many organizations still operate this way, especially those where employees operate in fear of losing their jobs.

Healthy organizations encourage employees to challenge the way things are done. It's not so difficult to do this when you've specifically been brought into an organization to make some waves, which often happens when new people are brought on board.

6. Judicious Turnover Improves Productivity and Market Leadership

Nonvoluntary turnover sends a message to those who remain in the organization. It lets people know that only those who are *fully* engaged and performing at or beyond expectations are welcome in the organization. This is quite a powerful message, and one that needs to be sent.

Those who've been hiding out will eventually feel uncomfortable. Most likely, they will leave before they are asked to do so, which in the end is a good thing. And if they don't, you'll need to show them the door. Congratulations! You've just set a new standard and you've raised the bar. Now go find some exceptional high jumpers to replace those who have departed.

Rule of Attraction

Examine the rate of employee turnover in your organization and compare this number to industry standards. If it's too low, then put a plan in place to shake things up.

Releasing Employees Who Are Tethered to the Organization

One of the unpleasant realities of leading a business is that from time to time the job requires you to untether from the organization people who are unable to release themselves. Or, sometimes business needs dictate a reduction in payroll costs. In both these situations, the way you handle the dismissal will have a lasting impact on the employee, his coworkers, and even customers. How do I know? Because it's happened to me, and I can still recall what it felt like to be untethered and left to float aimlessly in space, with the mother ship galaxies away.

Identifying Those Who Need to Be Released

Many of you are so busy running multimillion-dollar, or in some cases billion-dollar, businesses that you rarely stop to think about what is working well in your organization and what isn't. Specifically, about who is contributing fully and who has stopped. It's easy to dismiss what we may already know, all in the name of being too busy to deal with matters, but, as you can see, this can be extremely harmful to the long-term health of your business. It's also easy to let loyalty dictate whom you will invite to stay and whom you will ask to go.

A Tale of Termination

One of my clients was stuck for a very long time. He knew early on that his manager wasn't working out. He did everything in his power to work around this woman, even though he was paying her quite handsomely. It wasn't until I arrived on the scene that this madness stopped. During one of our coaching sessions he revealed to me how stressful he found the situation. It had finally gotten to the point where he realized that neither he nor the organization could achieve their full potential unless he cut the rope.

I'm not going to tell you that letting the employee go was easy for him, even though it was quite obvious that it needed to be done. I coached him through the process, and he did remarkably well. He treated the employee with kindness and made sure she received the support she would need to land on her feet. Throughout the process, I could tell how heavily this decision was weighing on him. And even as she walked out the door, he wondered if she would be okay. I reminded him that when terminating someone became easy, it would be time to consider another line of work.

In the end, he knew it was the right thing to do. He's in a better place today and so is the organization. And I suspect a day doesn't go by that he doesn't ask himself why he waited so long.

All of you reading this book are human. As such, there is bound to be emotion and internal conflict about decisions related to the long-term welfare of a particular employee. If your stomach is in knots reading this, that's a good thing, as it indicates to me that you indeed have a heart. However, this is the time to set your heart aside and use your brain to look at the bigger picture and the general welfare of *everyone* in your employ. If you fail to do so, everyone may drown as you try to save a handful of people for the wrong reasons, and your business may be no more.

Here are some questions that I have my clients ask themselves to help them determine whether an employee has stayed past his prime.

In what way, if any, does this person contribute to the organization? **Or, alternatively, *If this person left tomorrow, would anyone even notice?***

I suggest questions like these because we often fear that if a long-term employee were to exit the firm, a backlash would reverberate throughout the organization. In some cases this is true. However, in my experience, the remaining employees say to one another, "Well, it's about time!" They then return to work as if nothing had changed. Perhaps they do this because it's true. Nothing changed because the departing employee hadn't been contributing for a long time, and therefore there isn't much to miss.

Has this person reached his maximum potential and can do no more?

At some point, it happens to many, particularly those who stop investing in their personal development. They reach a certain level in the organization and they cannot or, perhaps, should not go any further. Of course, we all know of situations where people were promoted beyond their abilities only to fall flat on their faces. It's fine to leave someone in a job, regardless of his tenure, if he is doing a good job and is growing with the company. But if you feel compelled to promote someone out of obligation, then stop yourself before you go down a slippery slope that may injure your company's reputation.

In situations like these, it's best to be honest with the employee. Let the person know she has gone as far as she is going to go in the organization. Remind her that this means that pay increases, if any, will be minimal. Allow her time to consider whether this is acceptable, and, if it's not, work with her to create an exit plan that will ensure a smooth transition for all parties involved.

This employee may have helped us get us where we are today, but will he be able to take us where we need to go in the future?

This is a good question to ask if your firm is scaling up for the next round of growth or if you are changing directions altogether. I always say to my clients that if I had come over to America on the Mayflower, I would have headed west as soon as the colony was established. That's because I'm the type of person who thrives on building organizations. I prefer to leave the maintenance part to others.

You may have employees who were exactly what you needed when you hired them, and they may have done a terrific job. But are they still the right people now that you are in maintenance mode? Can they take you to the next level? It can be hard to let go of these people because you feel a sense of loyalty, knowing you wouldn't be where you are today without them. That's true. But unless you are an employment agency, your purpose isn't to keep people employed, especially if you are doing them a disservice by keeping them attached to your organization.

No one wants to hear that he is being let go because it's the right thing to do for him. At least not when you are delivering the news. If this is really true, then I guarantee that in a few years' time, the employee will return and thank you for giving him the boost he needed to find a place where he could thrive once again.

Is this person still here because she wants to be or is she here because external forces say she needs to be?

I know a lot of employees who are hanging onto jobs so they can support their families. They sure as heck wish they could leave their employers, but if they do, they will face the wrath of an angry spouse asking if they've lost their minds. In the meantime, you still have a business to run. If you can readily identify these people, then it's fairly clear that they are simply going through the motions. They are doing the minimum possible to get by every day. Do you want these types of people interacting with your clients? Especially when you know there are many people who would give it their all to be employed with a firm such as yours.

Would this person be better served if he was doing something he truly loved?

I've been involved in enough terminations to know that sometimes people are extremely grateful that you've done what they didn't have the guts to do: set them free. When you release them from your company, they often return to school to become what they wanted to be all along, rather than working in a job that their mother or father thought they should have. Or they find work that is more in line with their calling. It's truly a memorable moment to see a tense face relax as you give someone the freedom he was unable to give himself.

What impact will doing nothing have on the rest of the organization?

I find that sometimes, just by asking this question, it becomes crystal clear why doing nothing is not an option. For example, if your response to this question is that competitors will quickly gain ground and perhaps surpass you, then that will likely give you the impetus you need to take action. Or perhaps you realize that if you do nothing, more people will continue to leave your organization because of their dissatisfaction with the company or your leadership. Others will be repelled based on the reputation you've now given yourself. List the effects that doing nothing will have on your business, and keep in mind that if your business isn't moving forward, you will fall behind.

How to Release People with Dignity and Keep Your Brand Intact

On *The Apprentice*, Donald Trump makes it look so easy. Call people into the boardroom and tell them, "You're Fired!" Simple and to the point, right? Then walk out the door and join your daughter and son on the golf course.

Here's the thing. Many of the people who are fired on *The Apprentice* go on to have their own television shows. This is most likely not the reality for your people. They will instead be forced to file for unemployment and, who knows, perhaps bankruptcy. Not a pretty picture.

Being fired can have an everlasting impact on one's self-esteem, even if you know, deep down inside, it really wasn't your fault. Case in point: there is no way that I could have been personally responsible for the downturn in the oil and gas industry in the early eighties, yet for years I reexamined every move I made at the oilfield equipment company that eventually laid me off. At the time, I had no choice but to set my ego aside and find a job in one of the worst job markets in the country. I did so and eventually secured a position that changed my life for the better. What I learned most from this experience is the importance of being humane when you take someone's livelihood away from her, even if you know it's the right thing to do.

Following are some of the many lessons I learned that day that have stuck with me for life. I hope they will remain close to your heart as well and that you will read this section again before you pull the plug on someone's employment.

Do the Job Yourself

A dear friend of mine shared the tragic story of how her brother-in-law learned of his termination when someone from the corporate office, whom he'd never met, turned up one day to tell him he was fired. This may sound familiar to many of you, as this was George Clooney's role in the movie *Up in the Air.* Only this wasn't a movie. This was someone's life.

I can't tell you whether this man deserved to be fired. However, I can say that no one deserves to go out this way. It may cause you discomfort or it may be downright inconvenient for you to personally get on a plane to tell an employee he is fired, but this isn't about you. It's about this person and the way others will perceive your company when he eventually decides to tell everyone what *really* happened that day. As for my friend's brother-in-law, he quickly received another offer from a company whose offer he originally declined. However, his life is now forever changed. I'm sure a day doesn't go by that he doesn't have one eye open for another stranger who may walk in the door to take his livelihood away.

Treat Everyone with Dignity and Respect

I'd like to tell you that the following story is fiction, but not even the best writer in the world could make this up. A national company with a facility in my community decided to treat a layoff as if it were a surprise party. Invitations were sent out weeks ahead to those who needed to be involved in the planning. Private conversations were held to make sure the "guests of honor" were kept in the dark regarding the event. Special gifts, also known as separation packages, were neatly prepared before the big day. And then it happened. A specific group was invited into the conference room and, like young children at a birthday party, they were asked to participate in a game similar to musical chairs. Only in this game, the people didn't get up and move. Instead, they were told by the "host" to feel for an envelope under their chair. They were then instructed not to open the envelope until they got home.

This might not have turned into a PR nightmare if the people in the room had been five years old and if the envelopes really had contained gifts that would make a child squeal. However, this was not the case. Being adults, many people opened their envelopes in the parking lot and began to compare severance packages. I imagine one "kid" was bright enough or perhaps angry enough to call the local newspaper, as this story made headlines only hours after the "party" ended.

Leaders often ask me if they should do layoffs in groups or individually. I ask you, after reading this story, to tell me what you think is the right answer.

Employee terminations should not be a surprise unless your company is forced to close its doors due to a natural disaster. If executives and middle managers in your company are doing their jobs and managing performance, workers should know exactly where they stand at all times.

If you find that terminated employees are surprised more often than not, then you have a different problem on your hand, one that requires immediate attention. Why? Because most people sue their employers for wrongful termination when they feel they've been wronged. It's their way of proving to the world that they were right and you were wrong. Employees who feel they've been treated fairly throughout the process are more likely to move on with little fanfare.

Provide a Soft Landing

Those who are departing your company involuntarily will likely find that it takes longer than they'd imagined to find a job with equal pay, especially in a tough job market. If at all possible, provide your employees with a reasonable severance package to help soften the blow and to allow them time to get back on their feet. This one act of goodwill will be remembered for years to come and will position your firm as one that takes care of its people regardless of the situation. Consider continuing to pay for terminated employees' share of health-care premiums for an extended period of time and offer some level of outplacement if you feel this will help those exiting to quickly get back on their feet again.

Be Prepared for the Conversation

You have a pretty good idea of what questions will be asked, so prepare your answers prior to setting up a meeting. In these situations, less is more. By that I mean that you've already made a decision and now you are there to carry it out.

The termination meeting isn't the time to go through the entire list of reasons that the employee is being released. That will only create confusion. Instead, summarize the reason for the termination and steer the conversation toward helping the employee process what's been said. Allow him time to collect his thoughts so he can leave the room composed.

If at all possible, avoid the "perp" walk. You know, the one where security is called to stand next to the employee while he packs his personal belongings. It's embarrassing for everyone. If you are at all concerned with theft of company property, conduct the termination after office hours and walk the employee back to his desk, even if it makes you feel uncomfortable. If in doubt, always ask yourself how you would want to be treated if you were in the other person's shoes. Keeping this in mind will guide you to do the right thing.

In the End, It's Not about Winning

The Apprentice is all about winning. But unless your organization is part of a reality TV show, there is no "winning" when you have to let a team member go. Your objective is to transition the employee out of the organization with as little fanfare as possible. This can be accomplished when you shift the power back to the employee.

What if, instead of firing the employee, you were to give him an option of resigning? The employee would get to depart on his terms and won't have to go home and tell his spouse he's just been fired. He gets to keep his dignity and, in the end, you get what you want. This employee is no longer part of your organization. Think about this the next time you are tempted to shout, "You're fired!" If you remember this is not about winning, you will have employees thanking you on their way out the door. Just like on *The Apprentice*.

It is critical now, more than ever, to be mindful about the way you treat employees who are being let go. Many will go off to start their own businesses and, in some cases, may return to you as a customer. Others will think nothing of announcing their firing on Facebook and on other sites your customers might be visiting. And sometimes these employees will find themselves employed by companies where you are bidding. What they have to say about you can either help or severely hurt your chances of getting the business. And lastly, if you live in a small community you will no doubt run into these people at church, the supermarket, or your daughter's dance studio. It sure would be nice if you didn't have to sneak around town with dark glasses and a baseball cap for the rest of your life, especially at nighttime.

Closing the Loop with Your Employees

During these tumultuous times, it's easy to forget about the survivors. These are the people left behind to pick up the slack. While the boss who has done the firing has moved on, these people have not. Many are keeping their heads down, waiting for the other shoe to fall. Some are wondering how those who were asked to go were treated, in case they're next.

What Really Happens When One Person Is Fired

My mentor Alan Weiss, president of Summit Consulting Group, says that whenever one person is fired, you actually lose *four* people.

1. The person you fire
2. The person who feels guilty that it wasn't him, and whose performance declines
3. The person who wants to avoid being next, and hides
4. The person who is excellent, and feels she ought to get her résumé out on the street

Weiss goes on to point out that the organization suffers huge productivity drops due to numbers 2, 3, and 4. In my experience, this is absolutely true.

It's critical to close the loop with those who are left behind. Any time an employee is let go, it's best to assemble team members *before* rumors fly. You *are* going to be asked why someone has been terminated, so you'd better have an answer ready. If it's purely an economic decision, then it's fine to tell people that cuts had to be made to ensure the company's financial health during these tough economic times. But what if the termination was due to poor performance or, even worse, illegal activities like fraud or sexual harassment?

Here is how I suggest you handle situations like this: "I'm not at liberty to discuss the details with you, but Fred Jones is no longer with the firm as of today. I'm not going to go into this with you out of respect for Fred and his right to privacy. If you have any questions as to how this change will impact your job, feel free to make an appointment with me to discuss this in more detail. Thank you for your understanding. So, let's talk about what we all need to do to ensure nothing falls through the cracks."

Handling employee terminations will get easier with practice. But the truth is, the day it gets *too* easy is the day you should give further consideration to whether you are the type of leader others would be proud to call their own.

Notifying Those Outside the Organization

Customers do business with people, and, for better or worse, the people they do business with may be the same ones that you've just let go or who have left your firm voluntarily. How you should go about notifying others that a particular person is no longer in your employ will depend on the situation and the position the employee held. For example, if a top salesperson has just left the firm, then it would be prudent for the VP of Sales to immediately call customers to reassure them that they are being cared for. If there is no one in this position, then it's best if you personally notify your most valuable customers of the change in personnel. It's not necessary to go into details about why this person is no longer with the company. Instead, focus on how you will be managing the change going forward and, if you have the name of the employee's replacement, make sure you make an introduction.

Be careful not to defame the character of those who have left your company. Doing so could put your organization in the unpleasant situation of having to deal with a defamation of character lawsuit, which can be quite time consuming and expensive to defend. It should also be mentioned that talking negatively about a former employee may result in others questioning your character. After all, what kinds of leaders publicly bash people from their own firm? Certainly not those who are concerned about preserving the magnetism and the brand they have worked so hard to build.

Rule of Attraction

Ask yourself the following questions to help determine whether a particular person needs to be untethered:

1. If this person left tomorrow, would anyone even notice?
2. Has this person reached his maximum potential and can do no more?
3. Can this person take us where we need to be?

Your answers will dictate what needs to be done next.

CONCLUSION

Throughout this book I've provided examples and ideas for you to consider as you work toward creating the type of workplace that will be attractive to those who feel the connection as well as suggestions for repelling those who simply don't fit in. The next step is to put your knowledge into action.

There is so much great talent out there waiting for you to pull them in. Doing so will help you create killer gaps between the competition and your organization, which in turn will allow you to continue taking risks and remaining in the enviable position of best in class. It's a position that is afforded to few, and it's one that is well rewarded.

As you work through this process, be sure you are doing more than just checking off boxes. Those of you who are fortunate enough to be in a meaningful relationship know that there is a difference between people who go through the motions and those who are there for you every day. Be the leader who is fully present for your people, and they, in turn, will do the same for you, your customers, and your shareholders.

To remain in this position, pay attention to the changing needs of your people. Those of you with a young workforce know firsthand how younger workers perceive health and wealth benefits such as disability and life insurance and, in some cases, even health insurance and that 401(k) plan you keep funding. When I was in my twenties, I didn't care about those things either. Now that I'm a bit older, I thank my former employer every day for taking the money that I would have spent at Club Med and instead helping me to fund what I hope will be my golden years. I'm a lot better off than many of my friends because of this. Continue to serve your employees well, and eventually they will thank you.

In science, magnetism gets weaker as objects move farther apart. The same thing happens in organizations, when leaders find themselves removed from their employees. Eventually, the attraction is no longer there, which makes it easy for a more magnetic organization to pull your top talent toward it. This is a costly and irreversible mistake, but you can prevent it from happening by constantly connecting with your people: by remaining visible, being approachable, and purposely staying near those you most value.

My message for you is to not wait until the talent pool tightens or the economy gets any stronger before taking action. Don't wait until your business is failing or your competitor makes a game-changing announcement. Building a magnetic workplace that attracts the best—top talent that will stick around—should be an initiative in every business, in any economy. Stick with it. Your efforts will be well rewarded.

REFERENCES

2012 Talent Shortage Survey Research Results, ManpowerGroup. http:// www.manpowergroup.us/campaigns/talent-shortage-2012/ pdf/2012_Talent_Shortage_Survey_Results_US_FINALFINAL.pdf

Andruss, Paula, "Secrets of the 10 Most-Trusted Brands," *Entrepreneur.com*, March 20, 2012, http://www.entrepreneur.com/article/223125.

Branson, Richard, "Richard Branson on Office Ties and the Company Dress Code," *Entrepreneur*, May 29, 2012, http://www.entrepreneur.com/article/223670.

Clarke, Sara K., "Rosen Hotels Debuts New Employee Medical Center," *Orlando Sentinel*, February 17, 2012, http://articles.orlandosentinel.com/2012-02-17/health/os-harris-rosen-medical-clinic-20120217_1_new-employee-health-care-primary-care

Cleaver, Joanne, "The Dirty Truth About 'Best Places to Work' Lists," MoneyWatch, June 28, 2010. http://www.cbsnews.com/8301-505125_162-44540189/the-dirty-truth-about-best-places-to-work-lists/.

Closing the Engagement Gap: A Road Map for Driving Superior Business Performance, Towers Perrin Global Workforce Study 2007–2008, http://www.towersperrin.com/tp/getwebcachedoc?webc=HRS/USA/2008/200803/GWS_Global_Report20072008_31208.pdf.

Feintzieg, Rachel, Mike Spector and Julie Jargon, "Twinkie Maker Hostess to Close," *The Wall Street Journal*, November 16, 2012, http://online.wsj.com/article/SB10001424127887324556304578122632560842670.html

Has the great recession changed the talent game? Six guideposts to managing talent out of a turbulent economy, Deloitte, 2010. http://images.forbes.com/forbesinsights/StudyPDFs/TalentPulseWrapApril2010.pdf

Rasmussen, Brent, 2011, "Employment Brand? Study Says Half of Companies Don't Have One," *TLNT.com*, http://www.tlnt.com/2011/08/24/employment-brand-study-says-half-of-companies-dont-have-one/.

Ready, Douglas A., Linda A. Hill and Jay A. Conger, "Winning the Race for Talent in Emerging Markets," *Harvard Business Review*, November 2008.

INDEX